LOSING IT

LOSING IT

Sex Education for the 21st Century

Sophia Smith Galer

Leabharlanna Chathair Bhaile Átha Cliath
Dublin City Libraries

WILLIAM
COLLINS

William Collins
An imprint of HarperCollins*Publishers*
1 London Bridge Street
London SE1 9GF

WilliamCollinsBooks.com

HarperCollins*Publishers*
1st Floor, Watermarque Building, Ringsend Road
Dublin 4, Ireland

First published in Great Britain in 2022 by William Collins

1

For Hanna Yusuf,
who had many more stories yet to write

Contents

Introduction

Would you trust condoms from Poundland?
17 and still a virgin, is it normal?
Can masturbation worsen depression?

No, I'm not the one asking these questions, though I don't necessarily know half of the answers myself. These are the subject headings of posts on The Student Room, the UK's biggest online student community and forum. Here in its sexual health chatroom lie the sexual anxieties of a nation's youth.

I can't squirt :/
I don't feel anything during sex.
This is a horrible memory idk what to do.
Which hole is it?

Your first question might be: *why are they asking strangers this on the internet?* But the better question you should be asking is: *why is there no one in their lives they can ask? And why do so many of them have questions that medical professionals, teachers and parents should have already answered for them?*

Seventy-five per cent of The Student Room are under twenty-one, so we know that these messages, almost exclusively anonymous, are coming from people at the beginning of their sexual maturity. We also know from research that people really benefit from anonymity online when they want to seek advice; it gives them a sense of security and safety, especially when they know they are united by a single identity, like 'student'. On platforms such as Reddit, a forum so popular it is now valued at $6 billion, the feedback that anonymous users receive when they disclose their stories in mental illness communities has been found by researchers to be highly emotionally engaging and helpful. It's clear on The Student Room, as well as Reddit itself, that young people are reaching out into the digital ether to find advice and support for their sexual wellbeing too.

Ah. Yes, about that. Yesterday, someone posted on The Student Room that they had never had sex and were anxious about things moving further with their partner. So far, penetration with fingers had felt painful – any advice for 'the real deal', she asked? 'I waited for marriage for my first sex,' writes one postgrad bluntly. 'Your virginity is your highest form of self-respect. It is a special gift that can only be given once. Don't waste it with the wrong partner.' Another user asks: 'Would you date and marry a girl with a body count over 10?' There are nice responses, but also dismal ones. 'It's disgusting to be this easy and open your legs to anyone and everyone,' replies an anonymous user, adding that her 'vagina must be the size of Blackwall tunnel now. I honestly don't think any normal guy would want to be with a woman that has slept around with everyone.'

I grew up hearing these things, reading these things and maybe – terrifyingly – believing some of these things. From a smorgasbord of the internet, TV and the girls at my school, the wealth of information about sex I could access in a digital era was greater than any generation before me, but it came at a price for all of us. Because alongside all the right information lies the wrong. With all the half-truths linger the half-lies and quiet malevolence of traditional social scripts. The sex myths that I unknowingly subscribed to went on to destroy my first sexual experiences and, as I've come to realise while writing this book, also affected some of the relationships I tried to foster long afterwards. I spent my eighteenth year viewing my body as a failure, slowly watching my mental health slip away with my self-esteem. Nearly a decade later, I think quite differently. I see some-one who *was failed*.

Dig deeper into the posts of The Student Room, and the questions young people have reveal a lack of access to the sex and health information they deserve. I took around 450 of their most recent posts on the sexual health forum and found that the most frequent queries are about contraception, masturbation, pregnancy scares, basic questions about the male and female anatomy, virginity anxiety, the female orgasm and pain or blood during sex. When I say basic, I really mean basic; lots of women have no idea how to insert a tampon, toy or finger because they haven't been taught about their own genitalia, or were chastised for even going near it. When men have questions about their anatomy, it's almost always about their penis size, because no one has stepped in to readjust their sense of what makes someone a good sexual partner – or interrogate why they feel like they can only be a good sexual partner in this narrow, myopic way.

The contraception section is filled with women who have come to the forum after negative experiences with the pill, and who are trying to have sex with bodies that seem to be fighting against them. Women who are asking why they can't reach an orgasm, or why sex hurts too much, come across as wholly unprepared for the sexual scenarios they find themselves now entering, as do the young men who are spiralling because they are worried they don't last long enough, struggle to maintain an erection or ejaculate too quickly. After reading through these posts, it makes complete sense that among sixteen- to twenty-one-year-olds in Britain, one in ten men and one in eight women have reported a distressing sexual problem lasting three months or more in the last year. Are we probing how much of this is down to existing systemic inequalities in the health system and wider culture – and how it's affecting their overall mental and physical health?

It would seem not. The number-one reason people seek out sex information through pornography and the internet? They '*didn't learn it at school*'. If you don't have the right toolkit to distinguish between good and bad information, reliable and unreliable sources, what's going to happen when you read comments telling you that you're worthless if you have numerous partners? What happens if you encounter pornography, which the British Board of Film Classification found was true for the majority of British teenagers, and you don't realise that half the stuff you're seeing isn't what actually happens between most people in bed?

The British National Survey of Sexual Attitudes and Lifestyles (Natsal) found that men and women who reported school lessons as their main source of sex education were more likely to be 'sexually competent' when they first had sex. This is social scientist jargon for 'ready', and the findings were especially true for young women. Sexual competence is the gold standard we should all be trying to meet; young people and/or the sexually inexperienced on the internet might be worried that it's their inexpertness, penis length, pubic hair, tightness or squirting abilities that are at the luminous epicentre of their sexual maturity, but they aren't. It demands nothing of our looks, skillset or experience. Instead, sexual competence the first time we have sex is defined by Natsal as a sexual debut past the age of sixteen, using contraception, which has a sense of the right timing and where both partners are equally willing.

Our sex education, as it stands, is a damning indictment of how poorly young people are meeting the basic criteria of sexual competence when they first start having sex. It is a tale of two halves, in a country whose curriculum has for so long focused on 'bugs and babies' – STI transmission and the prevention of teenage pregnancy. The result is that nine out of ten young Brits use a condom the first time they have sex, but nearly 40 per cent of young women and 26 per cent of young men don't feel that their first sexual experience happened 'at the right time'. Young women in Britain might not be getting pregnant, but the Natsal survey also showed that one in five of them say they aren't as 'equally' willing as their partners the first time they have sex.

We have fostered a society where condom use has been pitched as the best way to protect ourselves, with very little preparation on understanding what it truly means to be in control and happy the first time we have sex. When young people reflect on how well their education prepared them for sex going *wrong*, 42 per cent of men and 47 per cent of women wish they had known more about psychosexual topics at the time they first felt ready to have sex. Awareness about sexual dysfunction – be it pain, premature ejaculation or a seeming inability to orgasm – has still not penetrated the school curriculum, despite so many people asking for it when surveyed. As a result, many of these early problems are not only destroying young people's first sexual experiences, they are going on to affect their lifelong sexual function, wellbeing and happiness.

We need to be asking why young Brits are getting contraception so right, but why so many other things seem to be falling apart – especially in a country reeling from the kind of testimonies of sexual horror revealed by initiatives like Everyone's Invited, an Instagram campaign that exposed a culture of rape and assault across UK schools and universities. We need to comprehend the gravity of these negative first times, which are more likely to lead to lower sexual function throughout adult life. We need to look at success stories of happy, equitable sex, and figure out how it is we can get everyone there. The Natsal survey shows us it's not only gender making us step into our first sexual experiences on an unequal footing. If you're male and from a low socio-economic background, you're less likely to be sexually competent. If you're female and black, you're also less likely. If you're female and your main source of learning about sex was through friends and not the classroom, you are, again, less likely. And if you aren't in a steady relationship, or feel uncertain about your partner's virginity status, you are also less likely to feel confident and happy in bed. Combine this with the general lack of data on homosexual sexual debut, and the fact that we know some young people's sexual initiations happen because they are trying to 'test' their attraction or sexuality, and it becomes clear some people are simply more empowered than others when they have sex for the first time; a power and control resembling the power imbalance of our non-sexual social world.

We need to be intersectional when we probe our sex lives, figuring out how everyone can be given access to positive first experiences – and we need to hand them that knowledge in settings where they'll be taken seriously, and where they can take their teachers seriously too. Sex education could be the great social leveller, teaching its pupils so much more than just how to roll a condom down a banana and opening up a whole landscape of power, gender and sexuality instead. It could be doing so much better at stepping in and blocking the misinformation reaching us from the playground, pornography and plastic surgery providers. But as yet, it is not. 'Sex education could do much to debunk myths, discuss pleasure, promote gender equitable relationships, and emphasise the key roles of communication and respect within relationships to militate against sexual problems,' write the social scientists of the Natsal survey. If you are in any position of educational authority, this book asks – begs – you to take their advice.

As I found throughout my research, young adults are leaving school subscribing to a set of myths about sex. These are stories we are all familiar with: that our virginity defines us, that we are biologically altered by sex, that there is only one proper way to have sex, that to be sexless is to be unworthy of affection, and that consent is simply about the avoidance of rape and assault. In 2016, the *British Medical Journal* published a qualitative study on young people's views of sex education in schools, including those in the UK and Ireland. 'As I started experimenting and everything

I was like, I can't believe we were taught that this is not okay,' one student said. 'They didn't really help you with your sexual feelings, they made you kind of feel bad about having them,' said another. Reading through the responses, all I felt was a sense of tragedy. 'They don't really go into the whole relationships thing partly because I don't think . . . [they] want us to have relationships.'

The study concluded that sex education needed to be sex positive, delivered by experts and accepting of the range of young people's sexual activity. Other research demands this and is now being broadened to include topics such as sexual wellbeing and equity, which in a few years' time could start transforming how public health measures the quality of our sex lives. Up until now, populations have mainly measured their teen pregnancy or STI transmission rates. But social scientists are busy forming new gauges for happy sex lives, developing new criteria in which justice, wellbeing and equity sit alongside good sexual health. They will start asking us questions like 'Did you feel sad about a past sexual mistake in the last four weeks?' and 'Is there someone you can talk to openly about your sex life?' Some of this research will be coming soon, but a lot of it is already there – it simply hasn't trickled down yet into our curriculums or day-to-day conversations in the media.

A first-century story from the Talmud tells of Rabbi Kahana, a young man so curious to learn about sex that he hid under the bed of his teacher, Rabbi Abba, who later came in with his wife. After they had been frolicking for some time, Rabbi Kahana was so transfixed that he declared from his hiding place: 'The mouth of Abba seems as if it has never sipped this dish before!'

Rabbi Abba, appalled, looked down to find his pupil. 'Kahana, are you here!? Get out, for this is not proper behaviour!'

Kahana replied: 'It is Torah – and study it I must.'

I've not been hiding under any beds, I promise – but I have channelled Rabbi Kahana's curiosity, for our sex lives tell us a lot about the society we live in. I have been in a bottomless world of private Facebook groups, Reddit forums and Instagram DMs. I have spoken to everyone from a woman who sold her virginity for thousands to a man who gets paid thousands for 'repairing them', to pornographers, sex therapists and sex educators. But, most of all, I've just spoken to lots, and lots, and lots of people who simply do and don't have sex, and I've asked them: why? How? Why not? How did it make you feel?

With a mind to thinking about ourselves as sexually competent, and our sex as equitable, *Losing It* will, on occasion, make you lose it. I do not have a short temper, but even I have lost it sometimes, bamboozled by what I have found on Amazon or the misinformation conveyed by qualified doctors. It will make you more aware of how people's histories and backgrounds could be affecting their lives, and the importance of treating one another with empathy as we start unravelling the sex myths ensnaring our outlooks. Just as sex education has no GCSE, not everyone is taught the soft skills needed for us to broach these subjects with candour: being sympathetic, vulnerable and acknowledging where you've been wrong. In a hegemonic, masculine world, this is especially true of men. And yet it is men who often have the most to learn. More men than women in the UK wish they had been taught how to make sex more satisfying. Many of them might be surprised to realise that it goes beyond simple mechanics, to a more political and ambitious appraisal of cultural expectations. One of the best things you could do after reading this book is recommend it to a male friend. Recent research found men are 65 per cent less likely to read a book by the opposite sex than women are.

Before we decry the judgement, lack of education or misinformation handed to us by others, we also need to be ready to judge ourselves. You may already be debunking some of these sex myths without realising that you, too, have been perpetuating others. This is your trigger warning for the rest of this book, as well as a quiet plea to sit with your own sexual biography before reading this. Stories about sex myths inevitably involve pain and trauma. You may, like me, realise that the narratives of your past, which you had long whittled into polished anecdotes for parties and new partners, may not mean what you first thought they meant.

If I do my job right, you will finish reading this book armed with knowledge around sex, relationships and society that you have been both actively and passively denied.

I am not a doctor or sex expert – just a journalist who is used to reporting on the fault lines between the spiritual and the corporeal, the encroaching power of the online world and the deference that the offline world must pay to it. Though I am British and spend a significant portion of this book talking about research that has been gathered here, this book is global in its purview because we live in a globalised internet and multicultural world. While you might feel socially protected from certain practices or ideas, it is likely that the people you meet and work with, buy your milk from, receive DMs from and fall in love with may all have had their lives profoundly affected by sex myths, which took root thanks to appalling sex education, or a complete lack of it.

If you're in England, you might be fortunate enough to read this while benefiting from a new, more inclusive sex education programme to the one I had growing up. One that includes issues such as sexting and FGM and is more inclusive of LGBTQIA relationships. Annoyingly, a rather unhelpful pandemic has stalled this brave new world of supposedly zooped-up sex ed. But we need to make up for lost time. Lots of young people will have missed out on at least a year of sex education when they needed it most. And whether you are under twenty or over it, there are generations upon generations of Brits walking up and down the country who definitely weren't taught any of that at all. They have grown up in a world that obsesses over the loss of virginity and heteronormative, penetrative sex. They have grown up being judged on their sexual behaviour, and being taught to judge others. They have grown up in a world where sexual dysfunction is not openly discussed and where a health gap, an orgasm gap and an empathy gap have grown into a chasm between genders. And an awful lot of them are all trying to have sex – with themselves, with each other, and maybe even with you.

1

The Virginity Myth

'Every time you have sex,' I remember her saying, 'you will lose your special glue. And when you have lost all of your special glue, no husband will love you.'

As part of the PSHE programme at my school, external speakers of varying quality would be invited in to talk to us about sex and drugs. This woman, with an Italian surname and over ten children, was one of them. No matter that there were girls in the year group who were gay, or who had already had sex. No matter that the school spent the rest of the time telling us to study hard so that we could get into top universities and careers. All that ambition and awareness dissolved in front of this woman's formidable command of the room, because *no husband was going to love us if we were special-glueless.*

I wish I could tell you that her comments didn't leave a mark on me. I know that they didn't affect lots of the girls in the year, who sniggered, laughing her archaism off for what it was. Maybe it was because she was Catholic like me, with Italian family like me, that her words were imprinted firmly on my mind. All I know is that, in among the other sex education I had access to at school – free cinema tickets if we took chlamydia tests, and being given condoms – the Special Glue woman solidified the idea that sexual promiscuity was shameful, that my virginity was one of the most valuable things I possessed, and that my future sexuality was my husband's, and not mine.

The Special Glue woman is an example of how much female virginity, and its inherent value, is an idea that still pervades our society. You don't have to look at a not-even-that-religious school's external speaker list to find this messaging; you can just search Twitter or Facebook posts, read the press or go to the cinema. Those of us who fangirled over *Twilight* absorbed the messaging that Bella Swan's virginity is of value to Edward Cullen, who forbids sex until marriage. Virginity loss is transformative, turning her from a virginal, weak human into a sexed, powerful vampire, forever unable to return to her human form. You may have also listened to the song 'Fifteen' from Taylor Swift's second album, in which she sings the lyrics: 'Abigail gave everything she had / To a boy who changed his mind / And we both cried.' You may now be observing the fractious midlife of popstar Britney Spears, whose virginity preservation was met with so much media fascination that the Church of England called her a role model. Or maybe you were still at school yourself when the *Sun* counted down the week leading up to Emma Watson's and Charlotte Church's sixteenth birthdays, eager to cash in on readers' lascivious imaginings of the 'barely legal'. How many of us can recall older men asking us if we were virgins or not, who wanted to hear us mutter 'yes'? How many saw our sexual inexperience as relational to their sexual urges, irrespective of our own? This virginity obsession surrounds us, impeding what could be an easy, equitable journey into sexual maturity.

You might have grown up being told virginity was a 'social construct', or that it wasn't a 'real' thing. But if you were, you grew up with enormous privilege. Many countries around the world still hold majority populations that condemn premarital sex, and women's sexual freedom with it. Policing female sexuality and endorsing concepts like virginity usually go hand in hand, and even those of us who no longer have to bear the weight of this sort of performed sexlessness may still experience the vestigial consequences of an era that once punished us too. Modern sex educators now know to use other phrases about first-time sex – sexual debut or initiation – but many don't understand the reasons why it is important to do so. Needless to say, even those of us who think we speak about first-time sex in an open-minded way are still probably quite close-minded about what the definition of virginity loss actually is, which is something we will unpack in more detail in Chapter 4. In limited curriculums that don't have the time or funding to explain how power and gender affect our sex lives, there is often little room for addressing the virginity myth head-on – the idea that virginity still attributes value to women. It is a myth that went on to fill my own head with life-altering misinformation around sex, and that will undoubtedly have affected women in your life too. At its most mercenary and extreme, virginity's value is economic, applied to porn stars, prospective brides, sex workers and trafficking victims. More commonly, it holds a spiritual and cultural value, portraying some women as worthier of a relationship, marriage, employment and even justice in a world that might promise sexual freedom, but still slut-shames.

All these values uphold the myth that our identity or status is transformed by first-time sex, as if we really do climb into that bed one person and out another. Not only is that ridiculous – were you a different person before you ate your first tomato, or wore your first pair of gloves? – but our sex lives shouldn't define our access to acceptance, autonomy and justice.

You might think that at this point in the twenty-first century, the concept of virginity and its associated values might not really affect young women anymore. I get no pleasure in telling you that it very much does. For the past year I have received countless direct messages and anonymous posts from young women in the UK and abroad who have been led to believe that their first sexual experience could transform the outcome of their lives forever. This chapter, and the following two on the hymen and tightness, paint a portrait of a world in which the mythical status of female virginity continues to negatively affect women, and men, around the world.

*

In the Brazilian healthcare system, the Sistema Único de Saúde, Ana is entitled to three forty-minute psychiatry sessions a month for her bipolar disorder. Those sessions enable her, most of the time, to access some semblance of a normal, happy life. But lately, it's been getting harder. Brazil has the second-highest death toll worldwide from the coronavirus pandemic, and her family is poor. She needed help to begin with, and now she needs *more* help. She hasn't got any money, but she has something else that she thinks might be of value – her virginity.

'Last night I realised something,' she writes in an anonymous, now-deleted Reddit post. 'Man [sic] pay a lot of money for a virgin girl. I have a beautiful body, not Instagram perfect but almost there. I never had sex.' Reassuringly, she gets decent advice in the comments – namely that such an experience might make her mental health even worse. She replies to them quickly, and in one talks about her anxiety over the fact that 'part of the virgin fetish involves making the girl bleed, the pain that she will feel. What if the man hurts me on purpose?'

Ana sounds like she's encountered virginity porn, a niche within mainstream pornography. One of Pornhub's most prolific channels in this area, the Defloration channel, has videos that rack up to 13 million views in which women are made to spread their legs and close-ups focus on what's described as their hymens. The sex is then vigorous, forceful and, usually, involves the young woman screaming half with pain, half with pleasure. Go to free-to-view websites who don't have to satisfy the conditions of credit card companies, and virgin porn fills with bloodlust. On XNXX, a 'deflowering video' shows a woman's buttocks smeared with blood. Slightly further down, a penis is penetrating a woman whose vagina is emitting blood so viscous and red it looks like ketchup. Has Ana, curious about her body and what it means to men, seen these videos and felt their cold terror – long before she's had a chance to understand what sex is really like, and what it should be?

I message her after I find this post, which at this point is a couple of months later. She tells me that she's decided not to sell her virginity for three reasons. First, her Catholic faith condemns sex work and extramarital sex. Secondly, she told her mother, who cried and made her promise never to consider doing such a thing. And thirdly, her Reddit post opened up an alternative opportunity – making money through sending nudes. 'After I posted that, a guy showed up in my inbox offering me money. I doubted but played along anyway to see what would happen. He offered me a lot of money for pictures and said I had to work out a way to receive money from another country. I made it clear that I would only send a photo after receiving the money. Of course, as I expected, it was a lie. After that he disappeared, but I want to find another man, one true to his word, to do the same thing: pics and talking in exchange of money.'

Ana's story is but one in the virginity economy that continues to exist into the 2020s. Tales about online virginity auctions have featured in the British tabloid media for decades now; even suspect auction sites alleging to sell women's virginities for millions claim column inches in media outlets such as the *Daily Mail*, who not only fail to do due diligence on them, but also fetishise the 'proven' virginities of such women, who have somehow obtained certificates from medical professionals. The articles, going by their comment sections, enjoy the novelty of clickbait popularity. There is no discussion of how virginity is a social construct, how these doctors are carrying out a human rights abuse, and how well these women are protected. Who cares, when virginity wins so many clicks, boosting the site's ad revenue?

One woman I speak to, Lilly, sold her virginity online four years ago for €9,000 in Germany – enough for her to pay off her debt, but not remotely near the sums that the websites covered by the media suggest. When the requests started coming through, she had to ignore the vast majority because they didn't want to wear a condom. In order to appear on the website's auction platform in the first place, she was required to 'interview' with the owners, who got her drunk and forced her into sex games to make sure that she was 'ready'. Once auctioned off, she had to give the website 15 per cent commission. Both she and the website profited from the economic value that her virginity held – but who really had the power here?

Virginity's mythical value is one whose benefits are enjoyed by the powerful, not powerless. From certain brothels in Cambodia where virgin sex is considered to have anti-ageing properties, to Peru's illegal gold mining region where it is believed by some miners that sex with a virgin will help you find gold, it is the sex traffickers who profit monetarily, and the male buyers who profit corporally. Our languages enshrine virginity's role as a commodity; in English, virginity is lost or taken, for one-time use – a perishable good. There is the odd language that is different; in Swedish, virginity is dropped, as if you might be able to pick it back up again. But everywhere else, it seems forever gone; in Arabic you may not only lose it, you also might *kasar* it – break it. In Urdu, the verb for to lose that they use is not *gomana*, like if you lose a pencil; it is *kohna*, used if you lose something in an abyss or lose direction in life. Even our euphemisms in English for virginity loss – deflowering, popping or busting a cherry – denotes fruit or a flower that is ripe for the taking, and consumed without trace.

This value impacts women far beyond the world of sex work and trafficking. Bride prices, practised by millions of people, where grooms pay the bride's family for the honour of marrying her, still alter in value depending on the bride's virginity status in many countries and diasporas: 'What I am going to say will shock people,' tweeted Reno Omokri, a Nigerian former presidential aide, in November 2020. 'Scripturally, Bride Price is ONLY paid for virgins. Don't argue with me. Argue with God. See Exodus 22:16-17. By virtue of Scripture (and also in traditional African society), you pay no Bride Price for non-virgins.'

Reno Omokri ✓ ·
@renoomokri ...

What I am going to say will shock people. Scripturally, Bride Price is ONLY paid for virgins. Don't argue with me. Argue with God. See Exodus 22:16-17. By virtue of Scripture (and also in traditional African society), you pay no Bride Price for non virgins

#RenosNuggets #EndSARS

5:33 AM · Nov 7, 2020 · Twitter for iPhone

1,980 Retweets   **588** Quote Tweets   **5,872** Likes

Why might a woman be of less bridely value if she isn't a virgin? It's not simply a matter of 'purity'. A study in Ghana from 2018 might explain it a little; it found that male and female interviewees believed bride price was necessary for achieving desired masculinity and femininity in Ghana. The women saw it as bestowing respect and dignity in marriage, and men saw not paying a bride price as undermining their dominance in marriage. 'Having a bride-priced wife was seen as a masculine accomplishment,' writes the author. 'We also found that paying the bride price meant there was an implicit moral obligation on a woman's part to respect and obey her husband's commands and wishes.' A virginal bride, then, is a status symbol that represents a guarantee that a wife will be submissive.

On Twitter, Reno Omokri's tweet received both support and criticism. But the majority of those who responded agreed with Omokri. Someone with 30,000 followers tweeted in reply: 'if my to-be wife no be virgin, I dey reduce the bride price by 50 per cent [sad face emoji]', to which a man with 16,000 followers responded, 'I no go pay bro.'

Whether it's on the internet, in a tabloid article or in gossip from neighbours, we are frequently reminded of how much more positively virginal women may be looked at than non-virginal, not only in conservative communities, but also in more liberal ones. Seven years ago, an eighteen-year-old on The Student Room said that they were thinking of breaking up with their girlfriend because: 'I think the problem with her not being a virgin is that . . . I just can't stop thinking about the fact that someone else has "spoilt" her.'

I, as well as several of my friends, can remember being told by men that they were happy they were our 'firsts', as if we had bestowed a great honour or gift on them, which had explicitly led to increased sexual enjoyment. Did they, too, think other women were somehow spoiled? These young men were not sexually illiberal themselves, so why the archaism? And – hauntingly – why were our virginities, either in our own performances of sexual inexperience, or simply their perceptions of it, part of our appeal well into the twenty-first century?

*

There was another, different response to Reno Omokri's tweet, hidden among its many replies: 'And what about men . . . if men have had premarital sex, what makes them worthy of marrying a virgin? . . . Did God give details about this too?'

It is safe to say that we all come from cultures in which religious ideology has influenced society. In secular countries, this influence does not simply disappear overnight, and for the 84 per cent of today's global population who continue to follow a religion, influence is not disappearing but very much alive. While the world's largest religions usually demand chastity for men and women, there is a catch; in lived practice, religious ideology is often responsible for demanding virginity more from women than of men. The double standards can be found in the figures who fill their sacred texts. Take orthodox Christianity, for example, in which sex is only acceptable within marriage and for the purpose of procreation. Both men and women are supposed to adhere to this doctrine; and yet, male virgins don't seem to be fetishised for their virginal status, or have their sexual history engulf their identity. For female virgins, it happens as early as Genesis, where Rebecca is described to the wife-hunting Isaac as 'very fair to look upon, a virgin, neither had any man known her'.

In Catholicism, female virginity is prized in the cult of the Virgin Mary, labelled by Simone de Beauvoir 'the supreme victory of masculinity' – perfect mother, perfect celestial bride and perfect virgin, all perfectly impossible mutual identities for actual women. The Catholic Church specifically insists in its doctrine that she remained *perpetually* virginal, long after Christ's birth, and this subsumes her identity in a way that jars with how celibate men are referenced in Christian teaching. Although Jesus' chastity is also celebrated, nobody says 'the Virgin Jesus'. In Talmudic literature, virgins are entitled to increased alimony in the event of a divorce, which is double that of a widow's; no similar privilege exists for male virgins. In Deuteronomy 22:17, a story is told of a man who wrongfully accuses his wife of having sex before marriage. Her bloodstained wedding-night sheet is shown to the elders of the town to exonerate her. In accordance with Jewish law, the man pays a fine to his wife's father and is forced to remain married to her for the rest of his life. I'm sure that goes down well with the wrongfully slandered woman at the heart of this.

In Islam, the Hadith describes Muhammad asking a companion why he married a divorcee instead of a virgin with whom 'he could sport'. The Qur'an also speaks of a paradise where good Muslim men will be able to enjoy maidens who are 'chaste, restraining their glances, whom no man or jinn before them has touched' [55:56]. Similar comments are not made about men. Meanwhile in Hinduism lie stories in which the heroines of Sanskrit epics have to walk through fire unscathed to prove their chastity, and legends like that of Draupadi, who walks through fire five times to become a virgin again for each of her five husbands. Across all the faiths, women's virginity has mattered more than men's.

As these religions grew and blended with culture and society, stories perpetuating these double standards continued. When Christianity blossomed in Europe, so too did the stories of female saints whose virginity played such a seismic role in their sainthoods that they are literally known as the Virgin Saints, cruelly martyred by pagan Romans who wanted to have sex with them but were rebuffed because they were 'brides of Christ'. Christian literature documents over fifty of them and they are some of the faith's most blood-soaked stories. Agatha in Sicily rejects the advances of the proconsul Quintiliano because she has promised her virginity to Christ in heaven. Quintiliano responds by imprisoning her in a brothel, torturing her and chopping off her breasts in fury. Women like Agatha became patron saints whose stories were taught in churches; they were heralded as heroines and used as examples of idealised female identity to young women. If Agatha can keep it in her pants in the face of Roman torture, then *you* can too.

But where are the male virgin saints? Heroic stories about them are few and far between. One exception is Sir Lancelot's son, Galahad. In the Arthurian quest for the Holy Grail, the cup that Jesus was said to drink from during the Last Supper, it is only Galahad who can actually claim it because he is a virgin. It is more common for men to be born *of* virgins than to be remarked on for being virgins themselves; this includes Jesus Christ but also Alexander the Great and the twins Romulus and Remus. Romulus ended up killing his brother and sanctioning the rape of the Sabine women to boost Rome's population; he didn't need to be an innocent virgin to be remembered by history. To be a masculine hero, other qualities are demanded of you – often triumph and virility.

One may wish to be wary of accepting virginity's place in a religious world when it is neither policed nor promoted in a gender-equal way and does more to perpetuate patriarchy than simply enable living out one's faith. In 2014, Pew Research Centre's Global Morality survey found that plenty of countries around the world still possess majority populations that disapprove of premarital sex – especially Muslim-majority countries. One of those countries is Indonesia, where 97 per cent of the population disapproves of it, and where the army has just announced that it has bowed to pressure from human rights groups to change its rules so that female soldiers no longer have to take virginity tests to join the army. Male soldiers have never had to take them. Another of these countries, Turkey, was forced to issue a decree in 2002 banning virginity testing after their health minister tried to bring in a rule that midwife and nursing students should be virgins. Again, male nurses were never expected to be subjected to these. But chastity was deemed a quality that would make these women better soldiers, better nurses and better midwives to such a degree that the highest legislators in their respective lands considered them.

So, what is the effect of growing up around the idea that you're only worth as much as your sexual status, because your religion – the moral code you and your community cling to – told you so? The USA gives us a lot of insight. Blair, who grew up homeschooled in the US, was only able to truly take stock of her upbringing in her twenties when she finally sought the help of a sex educator. She grew up in a Southern Baptist community, where she was taught things like 'sex before marriage is a sin that grieves the heart of God' or that it was 'the sin next to murder'. Blair can remember times when the boys would be told to go outside and play sports and the girls would be kept in and taught about virtue and securing a future husband. 'We were responsible for keeping ourselves in check and not being too flirtatious or dressing even slightly immodestly because guys are more visual. Guys can't control their thoughts.'

Blair went to these lessons for the duration of her high school years, and continued taking part in ministry groups at college. 'I really latched onto purity culture because I wanted to please God so much. It made me really sick; I was mentally very ill. I don't think I realised how unwell I was until the past couple of years. I did some really wild things.' She looks at the ceiling, unwilling to elaborate. Then she says, 'I remember the first time I held hands with a guy when I was eighteen. I cried so hard because I thought I had cheated on my future husband.

'The first time I made out with a guy, I was so afraid of being pregnant I went to the pharmacy the next morning and bought the morning-after pill. I took medicine that I didn't even need because I was so afraid I could have been pregnant.'

This is American purity culture's sad legacy. The kind of experience that Blair is describing is what happens when you

teach young women that their virginity is the most important thing about them. It is not unwise to teach young people
about delaying their first sexual experience, but abstinence
education doesn't tell young people that they need to be
sexually mature or aware before they have sex – it tells them
that there needs to be a ring on their finger. Theoretically
speaking, you could be nineteen years old and married, but
completely sexually incompetent. Blair wasn't even trying
to have sex – she was just trying to experiment and build
intimacy with men and explore her sexuality. But the idea
that sex was a seismic, life-changing sin that would doom
her was so terrifying that it had started to affect her mental
wellbeing and ability to generate that very intimacy that
could lead to romance and/or marriage, if she so wished.

I have spoken to dozens of young people in the UK
whose faith schools have taught abstinence, and they too
have felt like their teaching has been explicitly gendered
to highlight the importance of female virginity, and how
girls should guard it against lascivious boys. Troublingly, we
have not done the same soul searching in the UK that has
been done in the US around purity culture, nor have we
conducted much research into abstinence-only education
in a British context. We might not have felt that kind of
culture so deeply, but it nonetheless touched us. Countless interviewees have told me how this has affected their
actual sex lives, including one woman whose partner told
her 'you can't get into heaven now' when they had sex for
the first time, and a girl who spent the next day crying in

the nurse's office because she thought 'something had been taken from me'. In some cases, this is reinforced by actual learning resources, never mind errant external speakers; in early 2021, the *i* newspaper reported that over forty-three primary and thirteen secondary schools in the Archdiocese of Cardiff and at least one school in England were teaching from *A Fertile Heart*, a Catholic relationships and sex education programme, which teaches that contraception is 'wrong' and that 'looking at things biologically, it does appear that man has been created to be the initiator in sexual relationships, and woman the receiver-responder'.

At the time, the education campaigns manager at Humanists UK described education of this nature as negatively impacting young people's sexual outcomes. Is that statement unfairly attacking a religious attitude people are entitled to have, or did they have a point? In the mid 2010s the writer Vicky Walker created a survey to interview Christians across the UK about their attitudes towards sex, and many of the 1,447 responses were damning. 'I felt betrayed by Christian culture,' wrote one. 'I was completely unequipped to deal with a relationship in a physical sense once I started one.' Another said, 'My life was worthless for two years after I lost my virginity.' Only 13 per cent of the respondents said that their romantic lives had been 'straightforward and happy' – so much for virginity leading to a stable marriage.

Countries around the world teach this; in the summer of 2021, an Australian Anglican school was outed for teaching boys in a Christian studies exercise to choose the qualities they looked for in a girl, from a list that allocated more points for virginity, looks and strong Christian values. In the US, abstinence-only sex education enjoyed federal funding for decades. Five out of the last six presidents before Joe Biden have supported abstinence-only sex education and during the 90s and 2000s over $2 billion of federal funding has been directed to organisations that have advocated the wearing of purity rings and the signing of virginity pledges. Many of these organisations also subscribed to ideas that women's bodies are inherently evil because of their connection with Eve, that men 'can't help themselves' and that the only 'safe' sex is no sex. Research commissioned by Congress in the 2000s definitively found that abstinence-only sex education wasn't only ineffective, but could even cause harm by providing 'inadequate and inaccurate information, resulting in participants' failure to use safer sex practices'.

This kind of teaching didn't only endanger young people regarding pregnancy and STIs. Research from the University of Texas in 2017, which investigated the consequences of abstinence-only education for marginalised youth, found that this kind of teaching promoted sexist values. One respondent had been told that 'guys are like waffles and women are like pancakes because men could compartmentalise' and could therefore take part in sex without experiencing heartbreak and anguish. Another had been told that 'women are weaker, women should be taken care of . . . men go out and work, men can open pickle jars'. Three participants remembered playing shaming games in their sex education classes with M&Ms or Skittles where they had three minutes to trade their sweets with their classmates. 'Then they were like, "This represents your body or your virginity, and the more people you traded your Skittles with the more people you slept with.' In many countries around the world, props such as chewing gum or Sellotape have been used to show how, once your body has been used sexually, nobody else wants to use it. Some young people also get shown two pieces of paper, which are glued together and then pulled apart. Neither paper returns the same – implying not only that you're perpetually changed, but that you are perpetually linked to that original person.

Imagery like this can really stick – excuse the pun. That is why I remember the Special Glue speaker so vividly, despite being exposed to other messages around sex that were often far more open-minded. Someone like Blair fell through the gaps; through her church community she was exposed to ideas that posited women's bodies as shameful and sex as dangerous, and as a homeschooled child she was deprived of access to comprehensive sex education that would have challenged, or at least broadened, some of those ideas. In a 2019 study, women who had been exposed to shameful ideas around sex went on to suffer in their early sex lives. One said she wished she had been born male because she felt so miserable about her body. Another said that they felt ashamed and disgusted with themselves when they caught an STI, something that was reinforced by their family. One woman who'd been told not to get an HPV vaccine because 'you won't be having sex until you're married' never sought out any other information about sexual health because she thought she didn't need it. When she started to have sex, she realised that she not only had a deficit of knowledge, but also overwhelming feelings of guilt and shame. Another asked her mum if there was a pill she could take to stop her periods, and her mother responded by saying, 'Yes, but it's bad for you.'

As of November 2021, nineteen states in the US require instruction that teaches the importance of engaging in sexual activity only within marriage, and six require that only negative information is provided on homosexuality. Thirty-nine states and the District of Columbia require provision of information on abstinence, which is nineteen more states than those that stipulate contraception be taught. Blair is in a far better place now – she's had her sex education from a woman who runs a 'Purity Culture Dropout Programme' and lives with her partner, unmarried. She runs an Insta-gram and TikTok account, @talkpuritytome, where she challenges the teaching of purity culture – both the ideas she was raised with and the ideas that are still being taught today. On Valentine's Day 2021, she duetted a user who was decrying how many people would be 'premarital sinning' that day. Once, she would have agreed with them. But now, she knows that there is no longer a need to punish her-self for exploring her sexuality. Instead, she looks squarely into her selfie camera, and smiles. 'Oooh!' she sparkles. 'That sounds fun!'

*

It does sound fun – but that doesn't make it uncomplicated. In her book *Virginity Lost,* sociologist Laura Carpenter writes about one of the more confusing consequences of the sexual revolution. 'Casual sex was deemed acceptable for men,' she explains, 'but women were expected to make sex – thus virginity loss – contingent on love or at least strong affection, and preferably the title of girlfriend,' which invited many women to continue proceeding with caution about their early sexual experiences. Her words vividly reminded me of high school, where there was a similar pressure to partner up to find social acceptance, and to have sex with those partners and no others – otherwise the relationship wasn't a 'proper' one, and you might be labelled a slut by your peer group. Few say it better than Jessica Valenti in her book *The Purity Myth*, where she writes how we are often subjected to a cultural narrative in which 'men are masters of their virginity, and women's virginities are mastered by men'.

There is reason for women to proceed with 'caution', but it's not got anything to do with their 'virginity'. Take a heterosexual couple and sex remains a higher stakes game for the woman than the man: they are more likely to experience pain during intercourse, they are more likely to have been or become victims of sexual assault, and they're also more likely to experience feelings of guilt. They'll be less likely to know the detail of their own sexual anatomy and function than men are too. That's before we get onto the fact that they are also responsible for the physical burden of pregnancy as well as, often, hormonal contraception. Is it of any surprise, truly, that with all the gender scripts we hold around sex, women are less likely to have felt they were in control the first time they had sex than men are? As the rest of the book will demonstrate, these existing inequalities are rarely mentioned in sex education or even general conversation around sex; in fact, sex positivity and liberation demands that women and men are already equals when they walk into a bedroom together, and should be treated as such. Yes, they are, or rather they *should* be – but until we properly address what inhibits people from accessing equitable sex, can we actually *make* it equitable? If you're telling a young woman that she can best protect herself from harm by keeping her virginity for someone 'special', how do you define and determine what makes someone special in the first place? And who gets to decide?

The virginity myth essentially applies value to the wrong place; instead of applying it to a woman's sexual inexperience or purity, we should be ascribing it to equitable first-time sex. Articles, auctions and plot lines fetishising virginity and its loss would be more radical if they instead asked more questions about sexual maturity, probed how penetrative sex is valued above other forms and were more interested in how empowered young women are before, during and after they have partnered sex for the first time. Imagine if it were a woman's first orgasm that held economic, spiritual and social capital instead? Imagine if it were anecdotes of equitable sex that spoke of journeys, rather than single moments in which women are made women simply by the presence of a man, rather than as makers of their own destiny?

Laura Carpenter found that many women are told to see their virginity as a gift, and that it's a high-risk game; it sets women up for 'perfect' virginity-loss moments – loving moments, rose petals, candles – and gives them the expectation that they will receive something in return for that gift. Those whose gift-giving isn't reciprocated are sorely disappointed, and are left feeling exploited. Carpenter writes that many of those she interviewed who experienced this were 'unable to assert themselves in subsequent relationships'. If you are told you are made a 'woman' by a man during your first time, how much of the rest of your sex and social life is also shaped by male actions, male definitions?

I'll never forget studying Carol Ann Duffy's *A World's Wife* when I entered sixth form. I was left speechless by 'Little Red Cap', her retelling of Little Red Riding Hood where she meets the wolf 'at childhood's end . . . Sweet sixteen, never been, babe, waif'. The much more senior wolf becomes her first sexual experience. A dove flies from her hands 'to his open mouth / One bite, dead. How nice, breakfast in bed, he said'. The messaging around me, including a condom-focused sex education, really made me feel like my first time was something that a man would do *to* me, rather than something we would do together. It's only years later that I see how much damage this wrought on my own ability to understand what it is I want, and what actions I could take to manage my own sexual health and pleasure manlessly.

Others, Carpenter found, also contemplated virginity loss as the loss of stigma or shame. It's unsurprising that she found many men in this group, given men have generally not experienced the same policing of virginity as women, and have in fact faced the opposite pressure – to be sexually prolific – which I'll be interrogating in Chapter 5. But Carpenter also found a third, healthier outlook. Those who saw their first experiences more as a natural process, she said, were far more likely to have had comprehensive sex education and a slow and steady series of sexual liaisons before penetrative sex, be with long-term partners and be more accepting of the fact that their first time would probably be a bit bumpy and inexpert. Viewing first-time sex as a *series* of events, instead of a one-off interaction characterised by penetration, would relieve us of the idea that we change overnight, and that our value to others and ourselves changes accordingly. It would lead to happier, more equal and more autonomous sex. And as we will see in Chapter 4, it would also help sexual language be more inclusive of the LGBTQIA community.

Unfortunately, there is still a long way to go until we reach this halcyon world where our sexual status and a one-time event loses its value. For so many of us – including me – believing in the virginity myth precludes many other stories that we wrongly hold to be truths.

A young woman from the UK messaged me to tell me that, when she had sex for the first time with her partner, he didn't ask her if she was okay afterwards. He asked her if she was really a virgin. 'You weren't tight enough,' he mumbled, despondent. Then he asked, 'And why aren't you bleeding?'

2

The Hymen Myth

Este pañuelito blanco
que amanece sin señal,
antes que alboree el día
con flores se ha de coronar.

En un verde prado
tendí mi pañuelo;
nacieron tres rosas
como tres luceros.

This white handkerchief,
That emerged with not a mark,
Before the dawn light had risen
It had crowned itself with flowers.

In a green meadow,
I had my handkerchief.
Born upon it were three roses,
Like three bright stars.

So goes the *alboreá*, a flamenco song that is sung during the weddings of the Spanish Roma. Female virginity remains extremely important to Spain's Roma community; surrounded by the married women from her neighbourhood, a bride must lie down and submit herself to 'the handkerchief test'. This embroidered cloth is wound around one of the women's index fingers and is pressed onto the bride's Bartholin's glands, which are located at the opening of the vagina and lubricate it during arousal. Stimulated by touch, marks are left behind on the fabric called *rosas* – roses. This white-yellowish fluid is the bride's *honra*, her virginal honour, believed to reside in a small 'grape' inside her, which is burst during this process. The ceremony serves to deflower the bride for her husband – and if she is found to be already *abierta*, 'open', then the wedding could be cancelled.

This is not a relic of the past. If you search for it on TikTok or YouTube, you can find plenty of videos of families celebrating the virginity of their brides. In one video the bride is raised to her feet as the women sing and shower her with confetti after she has seemingly 'passed' the test. In another, the groom proudly raises the handkerchief in front of the assembled wedding party. When the marriage of Farruquito, one of the world's greatest living flamenco dancers, was broadcast across all major Spanish television channels in 2005, there was an outcry – the filming also included the showcasing of his teenage bride's handkerchief, marked with four *rosas*. At the time, the president of the Federation of Progressive Women in Spain said the test was 'indefensible, a disgrace that takes us back to the Dark Ages. To have to suffer such a public humiliation is surely in contravention of basic human rights.' But many Spanish Roma women disagree; it's simply *what's done.*

It's easy for many of us to question the belief that women have a grape – an *uva* – in their vagina, which is burst when they have sex. But the notion that a woman's virginity is somehow written into the detail of her anatomy is not simply something that is important for Romani people in Spain. It pervades the planet. Much like in Spain, it's crept its way into song and culture, poetry and prose. It is so well documented that it simply *must* be true.

The interest in the Bartholin's gland, however, is a bit unusual. For most of the world, it's not that gland but another part of the female anatomy that is associated with virginity. It's a mucosal piece of tissue, with no known biological purpose. When a woman has sex for the first time, this thin membrane is commonly believed to be ruptured, leaving behind telltale drops of blood on the bedsheets. Fear of prematurely damaging this delicate tissue is the reason why many women around the world do not masturbate, use tampons or ride a bike, never mind have sex. But this belief, and the fear that accompanies it, is unfounded.

In the twenty-first century, the hymen remains at the epicentre of violence against women. The myth that it defines a woman's sexual history consumes the globe, and a lack of education around it has failed to address the people suffering and profiting from such a lie. In some cases, it is passed on through the generations in seemingly harmless old wives' tales, but often, it is far more insidious. Sometimes it's the people we instinctively trust with the health of our bodies who are the most complicit in peddling such falsehoods.

*

'What is most fascinating about human hymens', writes historian Hanne Blank, 'is that we have become aware of them at all. No other species seems to know or care.' It's thought that aquatic mammals, such as whales and seals, have hymens to keep waterborne substances out of the vagina. Guinea pigs' hymens dissolve when they go into heat, and then regrow when they're finished. Our hymens, however, seem to offer no function. There is a hypothesis that they might help protect infant vaginas from faeces, which seems at least useful. But the truth is, scientists still aren't 100-percent sure. By the time we reach puberty and become adults, our hymens can vary wildly. Some are barely there anymore. Others might have thickened. A minority of women simply are not born with them. Occasionally, women might be born with hymens that do not leave much of an opening at all, either to menstruate or to insert anything, and so they will need a hymenectomy – a surgical removal – in order to have their periods or sex painlessly. The prevalence of this is small, but it's not insignificant either.

One British woman, Sophie, tells me how upset she is that she learnt nothing about the hymen at school, because when she tried to use tampons she would always feel pain.

Her mum's response was, 'You'll get used to it,' but she never did. Then, she started having her first sexual experiences and the pain was 'so impossible I thought a penis was never going to fit in there'. After hours of googling, she found out for the first time about the septate hymen, where a minuscule extra piece of skin grows across the opening of the hymen, dividing it into two smaller holes. 'I ended up breaking it myself,' Sophie says. 'I was too scared to go to the doctor, and I'd emailed lots of women who had written blogs about having one and they said it's common for it to just break during sex. I was far too nervous to let that happen, so I did it myself. I just wish I felt less shame about it, and that I saw a doctor.'

A number of my friends, especially those from more conservative cultural backgrounds, were forbidden by parents to wear tampons when we were at school because of the fear that a tampon would break their hymen, and then they would no longer be virgins. Our PE teacher clearly had no clue about this cultural belief, and would bark at my friends to 'go be a woman and put a tampon in' ahead of our swimming lessons. As a result, our beliefs went unchallenged, and misunderstood.

No one told us about the small study of thirty-six pregnant teenagers published in 2004, which found that medical staff were only able to make 'definitive findings of penetration' in two cases. Nor another study, also published in 2004, which found that 52 per cent of sexually active adolescent girls interviewed had 'no identifiable changes to the hymenal tissue'. None of this research seems to have made it through to sex education or popular discourse, and neither has research about first-time sex and blood. One obstetrician's 1998 questionnaire of her colleagues found that 63 per cent of them hadn't experienced bleeding after the first time they had penetrative sex.

One of the reasons a woman might bleed during her first time could be that the hymen has been abruptly torn, but she might also bleed because a lack of arousal or rough sex has lacerated her vaginal wall, or because the area is inflamed from an infection. Hymens are miniscule – there really aren't that many blood vessels there to bleed in the first place. A woman might *not* bleed because the thin membrane of the hymen has simply worn away with age, or because the sex was slow and arousing enough to stretch the hymen naturally and not lacerate her vaginal wall. Perhaps she wasn't born with a hymen at all. It doesn't take a genius to realise that in more conservative times, when society was largely clueless about female pleasure and girls were marrying with still childlike, developing bodies, blood on the wedding night might have been a more common occurrence.

In many cultures, examining the sheet to confirm the bride's virginity after the wedding night has long died out, though in some cases it wasn't that long ago. Even my own Italian family bears stories of it in the not-so-distant past. But in other parts of the world, such as in the Middle East, many conservative families still observe this practice. Few studies have explored the impact of ritualising virginity loss in this way, but there are a couple. A social study in Giza, Egypt, found that most women interviewed experienced anxiety and fear before their wedding night, and pain and panic during and after. A 2011 study of students at Dicle University in Turkey found that 72.1 per cent of female students and 74.2 per cent of male ones believed that the hymen symbolized virginity; 30.1 per cent of the men stated that 'the blood-stained bed sheet' should be displayed to the family on the day of marriage. In a Lebanese study from 2013, men were six times more likely to consider virginity a pre-condition for marrying a partner than women did, and 42.7 per cent of women interviewed said they would not have premarital sex for fear of not bleeding on their wedding night. Another study from Lebanon, this time from 2017, found that of 416 women interviewed, about 40 per cent of them reported having anal or oral sex to protect their hymen for marriage.

For women who do not bleed and are judged for it, the public shame could be fatal. In 2017, eighteen-year-old Rajabbi Khurshed from Tajikistan was accused by her husband, Zafar Pirov, of not being a virgin on her wedding night. Since 2016, medical examinations have been mandatory in the country when you register a marriage, testing for genetic diseases as well as STIs. It is common to also request a virginity test, which Rajabbi did and passed. Dissatisfied, Zafar Pirov demanded two further virginity tests. Zafar remained convinced that because Rajabbi did not bleed on her wedding night she couldn't possibly be a virgin. He raised it with the local community and demanded a divorce on those grounds straight away. And then, forty days after Zaraf Pirov penetrated his wife for the first time, Rajabbi took her own life.

*

The blood-stained bedsheet is one of two kinds of virginity test that are specifically connected to the hymen; the other is more commonly known as a virginity test, in which a doctor or elder inspects a woman's vagina and examines the state of her hymen. Despite the World Health Organisation calling for its worldwide ban in 2018, virginity testing is carried out in over twenty countries around the globe, including the United Kingdom where it has only just been banned. As I wrote this book – a year before politicians decided to outlaw it – I emailed a Harley Street surgeon about virginity tests, and his assistant tells me that I'd be able to get a medical report confirming I had an intact hymen after a £300 consultation, if I had one. If I didn't, a £5,400 hymen repair surgery awaited me – after which I would be issued with the same medical report. Hymen repair – which I'll go into more detail on in a minute – is a surgery that virginity test providers often offer, and which is now also getting banned in the UK. One wonders how many of these clinics might take advantage of women who have received little or no sex education.

A BBC report found twenty-one private clinics in the UK that offer virginity testing, which led to politicians backing a ban in law in November 2021 that would make it a criminal offence to offer someone from England a test, or help them get one in the UK or abroad. The UK charity Karma Nirvana said that between 2020 and 2021, they supported forty-one women where 'sex before marriage' was the motive for abuse from perpetrators. Some of these victims said that they had undergone virginity tests at the request of their parents. It is a small number, but still forty-one too many, and women often get put through them when their virginity has been called into question. The fact that there are British clinics and medical professionals offering the service only gives credence to pseudoscience. While testing appears to be established mainly in Asia and the Middle East, a wider number of communities than you might first assume may have people who strongly believe in virginity testing; in one conference I attended, a midwife spoke of being asked for a virginity certificate by a mother from an Irish Traveller background for her daughter. In Canada, a woman raised in a series of strict Christian traditions was dragged to a doctor the night before her wedding by her mother, also requesting a certificate.

Prospective brides and daughters are, however, not the only women worldwide who are subjected to virginity tests. During the Arab Spring, virginity tests were exacted on female protesters who had been in Tahrir Square. An Egyptian general told CNN at the time: 'The girls who were detained were not like your daughter or mine. These were girls who had camped out in tents with male protesters in

Tahrir Square, and we found . . . Molotov cocktails and drugs.' He went on to say that 'we didn't want them to say we had sexually assaulted or raped them, so we wanted to prove that they weren't virgins in the first place. None of them were virgins.' Why a woman's virginity would have anything to do with her right to freedom of expression is incomprehensible to most people, but in a country where a government was desperately trying to quell the voices of its activist youth, labelling its women as non-virginal was a deliberate tactic to terrify them out of protesting – and to caution any other women against deciding to do so too.

*

It was an otherwise ordinary Friday afternoon when Abir heard the innocent 'ping' of a new Facebook notification. She had recently started moderating a new social media account whose aim was to provide Arabic-language sex and relationships education. Arabic-language websites and pages about sexual health are few and far between; Abir and her team didn't really know what to expect, other than the unexpected. That's when she opened up the page's messages and saw several photographs of a woman's vagina – sent by the woman herself. 'Am I a virgin?' she asked, matter-of-factly.

'I enrolled in this as a journalist,' Abir tells me. 'I never got the training to deal with these kinds of things. Only a few weeks into the programme and this young Moroccan girl has the courage to take vagina selfies.' Even though years have passed since this happened, it clearly still stupefies Abir, who softly shakes her head as she recalls the images. 'A lot of women in the Arab world don't use their real names on Facebook, but you know, sending a complete stranger vagina photographs is a lot. She said she had had a relationship and now she was getting engaged and wanted to make sure she was a virgin.' Then Abir pauses, and grimaces. 'I hate this word. *Maftuuha* – she asked if she was that, she asked if she was "opened".'

The Moroccan woman who messaged selfies of her vagina to Abir did so because she would have been terrified of not bleeding on her wedding night. This educational platform, called Love Matters Arabic, runs a forum, *al-montada*, and they have over forty pages of posts in which people have asked for advice about the intactness of their virginity.

Is it possible to lose virginity by mistake or inserting a finger by mistake?

I read a lot, but I want a direct answer: Does a man's finger make you lose your virginity?

I am afraid that I lose my virginity once. When I woke up, I found two drops of blood on my underwear and I was itchy. I am afraid that when I was scratching the vagina I lost my virginity unintentionally.

I am in a state of intense sadness and worried about what I used to do. I used to put a piece of clothing or a pad and fold it and put it under my clitoris and then rub it, and now I am very scared that I lost my virginity. Please help me.

I want you to help me. I have my wedding at the end of the month, and I haven't got my virginity certificate yet because I'm afraid – I didn't have a sexual relationship but I used to masturbate for a long time by friction with the bed, with my clothes on. Is it possible the hymen was affected in this case?

What you are reading here are the anxieties that belief in the hymen myth leads to, from women whose self-pleasure and romantic interests have been paralysed by the fear that it could destroy their lives. In Arabic, masturbation is either *al-'aada al-sria* – 'the secret habit' – or *al-istimna'* – which essentially means 'to seek out semen'; the language itself drills in the idea that masturbation is something that only men do. Combine this with misinformation around the hymen and you start to understand why so many women are nervously requesting information online; Love Matters Arabic says that 86 per cent of information on reproductive health in the Arabic language contains inaccurate information. In one study from 2015, Swedish teenagers from immigrant backgrounds reported that they thought the hymen was a protective cover, 'totally occluding the vaginal opening, and that this membrane was to be torn during the first sexual intercourse, causing a bleeding which would serve to prove that the girl or woman kept her virginity up until then'.

As you might expect, the internet is also full of men asking questions about female virginity. On Quora.com, a popular question-and-answer website, someone asked in 2018: 'Would it be ok as per Islam to divorce from my newly married wife who did not bleed during sex on our wedding night? Can I claim compensation from her parents as per the Islamic law for hiding the fact that her seal was already broken?' On Islam Question & Answer, someone posts something similar: 'I do not know if she was a virgin or if something happened that I do not know about – Allah forbid – especially since she was engaged before I got to know her, to a young man who is known for his immoral ways such as drinking, taking drugs and committing zina.' Zina means – God forbid – fornication.

In the many Arabic-speaking forums that I found myself in as I researched this, I encountered a phrase that kept repeating itself: the rubber hymen. Shahad, a young woman born and raised in Baghdad, contacted me to talk about it. 'It means that the woman has a hymen, but that it won't tear during sex. Unfortunately, a lot of people use this as a sign to say that a woman is not a virgin, because she doesn't bleed. Some people go to the doctor to have it confirmed that they have a rubber hymen, that they're a virgin. I've heard stories of women getting killed because of this. But with a doctor's report, that can save them.' Another woman, from Egypt, messages to tell me that 'I would willingly sacrifice my Egyptian passport to leave this horrible culture,' alluding to its obsession with women's virginities.

Lama Abu-Odeh, Professor of Law at Georgetown, wrote in 2010 that, 'It is almost impossible to list the daily practices that are necessary for the construction of the virgin/female body in Arabic culture.' She describes these prohibitive demands as the public effect of virginity, 'an elaborate performance for the benefit of the social audience,' which actively polices it. For her, it's society as a whole that 'hymenises' women, monitoring their behaviour.

Any woman who has ever been told not to dress a certain way, smoke, drive, sit in a café with a male friend or ride a bike has been a victim of this social hymenising. It is brilliantly portrayed in the Saudi film *Wadjda*, where the eponymous protagonist is desperate to buy a bike but is told that girls don't ride bikes, all because of associations between cycling and rupturing the hymen. She is told not to laugh loudly at her all-girls' school, lest men nearby see or hear her. It's within the many social codes that women are expected not to transgress that Lama Abu-Odeh locates the basis of honour killing. 'A crime of honour can occur when any of the above borders is crossed. Killing a woman because she fails to bleed on her wedding night is one possible scenario for an honour killing. But a failure to perform honour/shame-based heterosexuality can be evidenced by far more minor miscues.' Being seen speaking to someone you shouldn't might be considered as severe a jeopardy of your hymen as an unbloodied bedsheet.

That was certainly the case for Israa Ghrayeb, a twenty-one-year-old Palestinian girl from the West Bank who died of multiple injuries in 2019. Thousands at the time expressed concern that she might have been killed by her own family members on the basis of photos that she had posted with her fiancé. Penal codes across the Middle East still offer exemptions or penalty reductions to murderers in cases of honour killings: sometimes just for the husband, sometimes for the husband and father, or unusually in Algeria, where honour killing appears to be a more gender-equal undertaking, both the husband *and wife* may be exempted.

Initiatives such as Love Matters Arabic, which boasts over 70 million video views since 2019, should be considered a success story. When you search 'virginity' in Arabic, their content, which challenges the hymen myth, is one of the first Google results to be returned. But some of the site's forums suggest it's not just the hymen myth we should be worried about, but the possible psychosexual problems that such myths lead onto. For women who have masturbated, one can only imagine the guilt that they might carry from going near a piece of their anatomy they've been told to guard at all costs – a guilt so palpable it pushes them to ask detailed questions on anonymous online forums, even to send complete strangers attempted photographs of their own hymen. Now imagine what it must feel like if you *have* had sex and you are about to marry into a family who expects to see your hymeneal blood. What on earth are you supposed to do?

*

The only interview I have been declined so far in the writing of this entire book is with an Egyptian surgeon who runs a Facebook group of 20,000 members. The cover photo is, for some reason, a pencil drawing of a werewolf straddling a woman who is lying on the ground. I can't quite tell if she is supposed to be defenceless, or in post-coital bliss – but the werewolf is definitely not the guy from *Twilight*. It's an image of unease, horror, maybe even rape. The group, in Arabic, says it will repair the virginity membrane – the Arabic phraseology for the hymen.

The doctor posts to the group periodically, answering frequently asked questions. 'How can you preserve the hymen?' he asks. 'Don't have sex and don't masturbate, especially not with your fingers,' is his response. He doesn't mention that masturbating by stimulating your clitoris and vulva doesn't get remotely close to stretching your hymen, nor that masturbation offers many health benefits. But elsewhere, he responds more fairly. When someone asks him if a vagina gets wider from sex, he writes: 'No, the vagina is muscle that expands and contracts to accommodate the penis, finger or fetus.' He decries the issuing of virginity certificates as well as the practice of 'pharaonic circumcision', the sewing together of the outer labia, as a form of hymen restoration. That kind of hymen repair would almost certainly be type 3 female genital mutilation.

Instead, the doctor recommends one of three possible surgeries. The first is laser surgery, which restores the tissue of the hymen, or more likely the inner wall of the vagina, reconnecting blood capillaries 'to ensure normal blood flow'. The second is a stitching job – a needle and dissolvable thread through the hymenal tears. Lastly, what he calls a 'temporary hymen repair', performed with a silk thread and laser. He adds that the marriage needs to happen within five days of treatment for this specific method to work. When I asked a gynaecologist why he'd use silk instead of the non-dissolvable thread, her eyes narrowed. 'He has probably said five days because after that the tissue would certainly begin to scarify.'

While there is technically no law that outlaws hymenoplasty in Egypt, the consensus (at least outwardly) is that it is an immoral procedure that would reduce the physician's reputation and standing in the community, hence why so many leave cryptic messages on Facebook in order to preserve their anonymity online. These local doctors' web presences contrast sharply with that of surgeons in other countries where the practice seems to be allowed to flourish. Although it is set to be banned, hymen repair in London's Harley Street seems to have cost women anything from £1,900 upwards. To give a sense of the profit margin some of these surgeons are enjoying, a freedom of information request revealed that at least 109 women underwent hymen repair in NHS hospitals between 2007 and 2017 (it's likely that such individuals took advantage of a loophole that permits victims of sexual abuse to have hymenoplasties paid for by the NHS). One of the trusts priced the surgery as between £630–£840, thousands lower than what many private clinics are charging. So how much of this is safe-guarding, and how much of this is profit driven?

Some of the prices are probably driven up by hymen repair tourism: young women from wealthy Gulf countries obtaining the operations during holidays where their family and friends cannot possibly find out what they are doing. At this point you might be wondering – well, at least I hope you are – is hymenoplasty ethical? Should it be allowed where I live? You may feel strongly about hymen repair tourism, in a way that you don't feel strongly about Turkey's dental tourism, or Iran's nose job tourism. Without regu-lation or standardised training, one wonders how effective the procedures actually are. A Dutch study in 2012 showed that seventeen out of nineteen women did not bleed during their first sexual intercourse after undergoing this recon-structive surgery.

Dr Lee Seng Khoo is one of the few plastic surgeons who has written publicly about the hymen repairs that he has conducted; he's also in the unique position of having worked in a variety of different countries, including Malay-sia, India and Brazil, where he was able to obtain training under more experienced surgeons. 'I'm comfortable talk-ing about it because we should address it. It's fine for us to speak openly, but I understand why some want to be low key. Many colleagues frown upon this practice.' In 2015, he and a colleague in Brazil wrote about the procedure in a medical magazine. They acknowledge the stance of the American College of Obstetricians and Gynecologists, who discourage it, but explore the dangers of outright banning the practice. 'By denying these women access to surgical treatment, are we also denying them their autonomy and right to live in cultures where virginity is an integral aspect for life and social acceptance?'

The article does, incorrectly, say that the Qur'an 'reiterates that a bride has to be a virgin'; in fact, the Prophet Muhammad had over a dozen wives and only one of them was a virgin. They would have been more accurate if they had addressed certain parts of the Hadith or cultural realities in Muslim-majority countries that go beyond the purview of the religious written word. They go on to say: '[T]he hymenoplasty procedure can be combined with labial trimming (labial hypertrophy being a mark of frequent sexual intercourse), vaginal tightening and clitoral dehooding. Hymenoplasty should not be trivialised as a simple, risk-free procedure that can be done by any medical practitioner. Legalising hymenoplasty can also put a curb on errant practitioners performing hymenoplasty in back door clinics in unsanitary conditions. The complications such as vaginal stricture, fistulas, infection and bowel perforation that may arise from hymen reconstruction are all real and cannot be downplayed.'

Labial hypertrophy – that means growth – does *not* happen when women have frequent sex, but Dr Lee Seng Khoo is not the first plastic surgeon I have seen online to offer labial trimming and other surgeries to women seeking hymen repair, advertising a whole 'virginal vagina' package.

There is no such thing as a virginal look or feel; simply natural changes that can occur from ageing and childbirth by which his clients, the majority of whom are in their twenties and thirties and from strict families, will definitely not be affected.

When he was working in Brazil, Dr Seng Khoo saw lots of patients who flew in from the Middle East. It is very rare for him to ever see them again as they will have returned to their country of origin to marry; the lack of follow-ups with patients once more points to a dearth of data on how successful or complication-free these procedures may be, though Dr Seng Khoo says he has received thank you cards. When he trained in India, he says that many women did not even give their real names.

'There are some peculiar cases,' he says, 'like in Brazil, there was an Arab man accompanying his girlfriend for a hymenoplasty. So he knew she was getting it. It was like a gift for him. There are one or two cases like this that I've come across.' In Malaysia, where he is now based, he says that the requests are low because of the pandemic, 'but just a month ago I did it for a girl who is getting married to a very pious Christian man, and she wanted to be a born-again virgin'.

I asked Dr Seng Khoo what the response to his paper addressing the ethics of hymen repair was, wondering if anyone, like me, had raised their eyebrows at his openness about it or the mention of additional 'virginising' surgeries that, just like hymen repair, have no scientific basis. He told me, 'When this article was published, I received about twenty or thirty letters, mainly from colleagues in the Middle East. They asked me, "Why are we deceiving people?"'

I asked, 'Deceiving their husbands, you mean?'

'Yes.'

*

In some countries, such as India, for example, you might be able to get cheap hymen repair from a beautician or nurse; it's cheaper because they're less qualified, and with that reduction in price you get a rise in risk. Women who can't afford even these procedures – or rightfully question how safe they are – may turn to artificial hymens.

On Amazon, I found a number of options available from a German-based company called Virginia Care. They are currently no longer available in the UK, but not because Amazon has chosen to take them down; Brexit has meant that Virginia Care can no longer deliver via their EU supplier, and so UK residents interested in artificial hymens have to order through their company website instead. Its branding is bright white and lilac, and the stylised flowers on the packaging make it look more like some sort of scented air freshener or washing machine tablets, rather than a fake hymen. *Your reliable way back to virginity*, it assures you, as it displays the products on offer. One is the Artificial Hymen Repair Kit – at £42 – which is a cellulose compound with blood-coloured powder that the woman should insert into her vagina thirty minutes before sexual intercourse. *The blood-like fluid is just as difficult to wash off from textiles as real blood.* Another product, its Hymen Blood Capsules, are see-through and contain what look like salt crystals or frankincense – they're brown and look abrasive. The website doesn't explain what they are, though presumably whatever it is dissolves and mixes with vaginal fluids to look like blood. The thought of Himalayan salt crystals grating inside my vagina makes my legs snap shut. At the bottom left of the screen, there's an option: *Chat with us.* I message to ask what the ingredients of the capsules are, and it takes me to a +66 WhatsApp number – a Thai dialling code. The company is listed on Google as a cosmetics wholesaler in Takhian Tia, Thailand, but the website insists that everything is made in Germany. Suspicious, I wait for a reply and keep browsing.

Other providers are just as nebulous. HymenShop doesn't say what's in their fake hymen at all – which is a little disconcerting given that it warns the user from inserting it any longer than twenty minutes before sex as 'it may result in the product losing it's [sic] form and evenually [sic] dissolve inside the vagina'. For $35.95, you get two – one to practise with, and one for the big day. In an article for *The Cut*, Leah Beckmann talks about her experience trialling the 'prosthetic membrane'. Though it promised to be 'Joan of Arc Red', it was instead 'like the inside of a lava lamp', 'the colour of cherry Kool-Aid'. My phone buzzes – it's the Thai number, which now has a name: Patrick. He responds simply by sending me a link back to the products. I explain again that the website doesn't list the ingredients, and ask if he could tell me what they are. 'No, sorry,' he replies straight away.

It is not unreasonable to expect the ingredients for these items to be clear so that women can make informed decisions about whether to use them or not – but I suppose that might mean the companies make less money off the desperation of distressed buyers. Another seller I find doesn't limit themselves to selling an artificial hymen. It encourages you to buy it as a package, which includes tightening gel and a 'Virginity Purity Soap', a 'naturally formulated blend of active enzyme crystals which fade the dark colours and brighten your nipples and vagina, restoring both to pristine pink'.

If you think Amazon shouldn't be advertising products that inaccurately suggest there is a virgin 'look', you have little recourse. The Medicines and Healthcare products Regulatory Agency in the UK can't ask for removal unless a product claims to do anything medical. But if it's saving someone's life, is the answer removal, or should we simply be pushing for more accurate information?

Calls to ban hymen repair are often simultaneous with calls to ban virginity testing, but the two are different. Bio-ethicist Dr Jacob M. Appel told me: 'The argument in favour of regulating against, say, virginity tests is that it is pseudoscience, which discredits medicine. But this is different for hymenoplasty. When you drive something like that out of the doctor's office, you could be driving them towards the people who are unskilled, who don't use a sterile environment.' He explains that you want to limit the involvement of a state in general in medical practice. 'My dividing line is when you want them to regulate behaviour that's demonstrably false. Where the science is true but values are different, you tread more lightly. If you ban virginity testing, you push the burden onto physicians. But if you ban hymenoplasty, you're putting the burden on the victim. She can't get a procedure to fulfil the cultural goals that she wants to achieve.'

*

The hymen myth not only perpetuates the virginity myth's inaccurate association between a woman's sexual history and her worth, but also harms women's access to owning their sexuality and demanding equitable, pain-free sex. The ethical ambiguity of doctors offering women what they argue can be a life-saving surgery needs to be balanced with good education and ambition. We all need to talk about the hymen more publicly, so that the myth can be eroded, but doctors carry credibility that is more influential. A doctor who tells a woman she is not defined by what's in her pants may help her teach her sons and daughters the same thing.

Many countries seek to ban virginity testing, but for some women, it is a sticking plaster for a societal wound that simply should not exist – and until it does stop existing, women will do as they have done for centuries. Survive.

It's in this spirit that you find several homemade solutions, which enable women to manufacture hymeneal blood if they are terrified of not producing a stained bedsheet. All of it involves an element of deception. Some women might prick their fingers; historically many have used chicken or pigeon's blood. Exactly how and where you would secrete the blood may not bear thinking about, though it's something that several TikTok users have started confronting, to thousands of followers.

@LadyTiramisu, whose real name I cannot share because she has received death threats, is a young Saudi-American woman who lives in the US. In response to a TikTok video she saw of a Romani woman proudly displaying a bride's bloodied bedsheet at a wedding party, she started making TikToks showing her experimentation with making a fake hymen that people could replicate at home. As showing blood on TikTok is banned, she fills small, dissolvable bags with coconut oil and grape juice and puts it in her mouth to demonstrate how, when it dissolves, it looks realistic. She asks if real blood would work, and wonders aloud in her videos (as do many of her commenters) if you might be able to freeze menstrual blood to save for the day and put inside the bag. It dissolves in her mouth after only two minutes – which might not be long enough for women who'd need to find a discreet moment to insert it before penetration.

When I ask her why she made these, she started reflecting on her childhood growing up in the US. 'Girls weren't allowed to do sports, have sleepovers, go out . . . boys were though. All the slut-shaming really bothered me. My older sister, who was born in Saudi Arabia, slut-shamed me really badly once. I no longer have contact with her.'

She can remember being a child and falling off her bike, and her father rushing over to her. 'Did you hurt your private parts?' was the first thing he said. 'At the time I thought that was super weird. But as I got older and found out what he meant, I just . . . it's so wrong. That shouldn't be remotely important.'

Her TikTok home science experiments have been watched hundreds of thousands of times. Amongst the minority of death threats are mainly messages of gratitude, with some critics. One woman, who claimed she was married to a physician, commented that using other blood would be pointless because hymeneal blood leaves a stain on a bedsheet, whereas normal blood doesn't. 'I deleted it and blocked her,' Lady Tiramisu says, exasperated.

But she is moved by the women who say thank you. 'One girl has just moved to Iraq. She's getting married and she's had sex before. She's sixteen. He's already said to her that he looks forward to, I quote, popping her cherry. She is so scared that she isn't going to bleed.'

I ask her about other TikToks I've seen, where the women use fruit juice. 'But dye and fruit juice don't dry like normal blood,' Lady Tiramisu warns me. 'Real blood oxidises, turns kind of brown. That would just stay bright red, maybe it would smell.' She hesitates, imagining the face of a stranger's husband, narrowing his eyes in disbelief. 'What if they can tell?'

3

The Tightness Myth

Sarah Walser was in the middle of one of her clinical rotations at Penn State University when she had to look twice at the note pinned up in her clinic hallway. It read: 'All rooms should have: two extra virginal, two virginal, eight regular, two long.' If you're like me (Italian and always hungry), you might hear that and quizzically wonder why a hospital would be so interested in keeping olive oil stocked in their consultation rooms. But the note wasn't talking about extra virgin olive oil – it was talking about extra virgin speculums.

A year later I sat down with Sarah over Zoom. 'I think they often mean paediatric,' she tells me. 'And it's weird because during the different appointments a lot of the time we use a smaller speculum for post-menopausal women. They have more atrophy, so it's more painful to insert things because there's less elastic tissue, which oestrogen provides.' As soon as she started looking into it more, she quickly found other examples where the word virgin was being used in medical literature. 'I didn't realise how widespread the term was and in different textbooks and also inventory lists for medical supply companies. They would refer to the small one as the virgin one.'

Nearly a year after Sarah wrote her essay, another young doctor in London, Millie, tweeted a picture of PELIspec wrapping, a manufacturer of vaginal speculums. Again, the product was labelled virgin size. 'What's wrong with the standard "extra small"?' she sensibly asked. Over 2,000 likes later, Williams Medical Tweeted in response, 'Williams purchased the PELIspec brand in 2019 and inherited the sizing conventions. The classification attributed to this size speculum is an historic name and used industry-wide in and outside UK. We acknowledge the challenge and are taking steps to make an appropriate change.' A few days later, they had changed their virgin speculum to 'extra small (previously known as virgin)' on their website.

As well as the myths propagated around the hymen, tightness too has been associated with virginity since time immemorial. This is why the hymen examination or blood-on-the-wedding-night test aren't the only virginity tests in existence; there is also the two-finger test, where fingers are inserted to ascertain the laxity of the vaginal wall. In the WHO's interagency statement on Eliminating Virginity Testing, they write: '[T]he vagina is a dynamic muscular canal that varies widely in size and shape, depending on individual, pubertal or developmental stage, physical position and various hormonal factors such as sexual arousal and stress.' There is no scientific basis for such a test or indeed the belief that the diameter of a woman's vaginal canal may reveal anything about her former sexual behaviour; yet this myth can be found across aesthetic, homeopathic and even medico-legal environments throughout the globe. It is also perpetuated in pornography, where 'tight pussy' has become a popular clickbait title for videos.

'There are tight women and loose women,' writes one Reddit user, before adding, 'the tightest are the virgins which do come with a tightness quality seal called hymen', as if women are some kind of household cleaning product. On an Instagram post where a woman is trying to convince a man that sex doesn't change vaginal laxity in the comments, she writes: 'A vagina is muscle. It is literally made to push out babies and they go back to their normal sizes. Do you really think that your baby dick will really have any effect on a woman's vagina if a baby doesn't? Read a fucking book.' He responds: 'Then explain why a virgin is really tight and a women [sic] that has 10 kids can fit a country up there? Ya cuz it stretches right. Any guy that's been with a hoe will tell you it's not the same as a virgin. So be gone thot.'

Perhaps it's also some of the nomenclature that's been misleading; phrases such as 'vaginal canal' suggest that it is a tube, when really the muscular system is more like a sock with folds and ridges that allow it to expand and retract. Childbirth and ageing can cause natural changes, but nothing of the kind that a) is being described and b) generally could not be supported by pelvic floor therapy. If this is the first time you're hearing that phrase – pelvic floor therapy – don't worry. I hadn't heard of it either, until I was eighteen years old, in excruciating pain nearly every night, and sitting in front of a GP. A lot of women don't hear about it until they're pregnant, and even then they may find little healthcare or awareness available about one of our most impressive muscle structures.

The tightness myth preys on how little we know about the pelvic floor and sexual pleasure in women. It comforts the insecurities of the heterosexual male ego, because dismissing the myth acknowledges that a penis or many penises do *not* change a vagina. Lastly, it makes a lot of people a *lot* of money. So, let's get started – and loosen things up.

*

If you are a man and you tell the women you have sex with, 'Oh, you're so tight,' you get five gold stars for unoriginality. As I have been writing this book, I have been reading Amanda Montell's *Wordslut: A Feminist Guide to Taking Back the English Language*. She writes about how when she was at college, her sociolinguistics class taught her how gender stereotypes lie hidden in English, 'like how the term penetration implies (and reinforces) the idea that sex is from the male perspective. Like sex is defined as something a man does to a woman. The opposite might be envelopment or enclosure. Can you imagine how different life would be if that's how we referred to sex?' I keep thinking about Montell's observation as I read descriptions of female tightness, and consider when I would actually use the word tight. I normally use it to describe the sensation of trying on a pair of optimistically sized leggings. And when I try to stick an entire Creme Egg into my mouth – again, optimistic – I wouldn't describe that as tight. I'd describe my mouth as being full. As Montell writes, this linguistically somehow feels closer to envelopment and enclosure, and what I actually experience when I have sex. I can completely understand how from the male perspective a vaginal canal may well feel tight – given the vagina has to stretch during arousal to make room for a penis in the first place, which according to current average estimates is just ever so slightly longer than the average vagina – but the fact that this word is now being employed by women in female health and wellness spaces as a desirable quality for the vagina seems to completely jar with what the science says on healthy arousal and pelvic floor movement.

Vaginal tissue is elastic by nature after puberty because of the production of oestrogen, but also because of the pelvic floor, the structure of muscles supporting our bladders, reproductive organs and our rectums, which act like a hammock. This big muscular sling, when happy, is what helps us not to leak out of our orifices all the time and works with our abdominal and back muscles to maintain the right level of pressure inside our core. Muscles can suffer trauma, especially during something as cataclysmic as childbirth, which is why in France all women are sent to see a pelvic floor specialist after they give birth. Some of us have over-active, 'hypertonic' pelvic floor muscles, which is when the muscles are so tense that they can't relax, and can happen to us for a variety of reasons, including working out your core muscles too much or not peeing when you should because you're afraid of using public toilets.

As women, what we might think of as 'tightness' during sex is determined by this pelvic floor. The muscles contract and relax depending on how you're feeling. The more aroused you are, the more relaxed you are – the more stressed, anxious or deeply unaroused you are, the tighter the muscle. When men speak of sexual tightness, they make it sound as if the vaginal walls create a cavity that dictates tightness as if it were a stiff sort of test tube, but it's not; it's the muscles *around* those walls that dictate tightness. If your partner likes it when you are in fact in a state of discomfort or pain, that is not what sex is supposed to be. You should be so aroused that you are self-lubricating and your vagina is stretching without you even having to think about it, like breathing. So it's with all of that in mind that we have to approach services that say they will tighten a woman's vagina with due caution, especially when they are targeted at women who are not necessarily menopausal or healing after childbirth.

It's out of this world that an online obsession with Kegel exercises exploded in the last few years, catapulted by a TikTok trend known as 'GripTok' where young women follow Kegel choreography through a series of sounds and emojis. Kegel exercises contribute to healthy pelvic floor function, but only within reason. 'Too many

Kegels can worsen pelvic floor function,' Dr Jennifer Lincoln, an American obstetrician-gynaecologist with millions of TikTok followers, tried responding to a number of the videos. At the time, she duetted one of the bigger accounts, saying that you shouldn't do these exercises without the advice of a pelvic floor therapist. A user commented on her video: 'I'm sorry but they make you tighter period. If it causes you pain at any point obviously don't, but why do I have to shame a fun harmless thing [eye roll emoji].' She duetted another video where a man says, 'If you want your pink portal to be known as the colossus of clam, we gotta do these Kegels,' before giving some exercises that he says will give you 'the ultimate gorilla grip'. In her duet, Dr Lincoln says that Kegels aren't about increasing a man's pleasure during sex. 'He's not even a pelvic floor therapist,' she sighs. 'He's an athletic trainer.'

Dr Lincoln is also troubled by the number of vaginal tightening products – suppositories and 'yoni pearls' – she sees online. 'They're from sketchy companies, they cause way worse problems. I ask, why do you think it needs to be tighter? You're playing into the narrative and they're profiting off making you feel a certain way. What bothers me so much is that it's other girls who are putting this stuff forward!'

Yoni tightening products have emerged with the popularisation of wellness culture. Yoni is Sanskrit for womb, and can be found referred to across a number of spiritual spaces around the world, including Hollywood wellness companies such as Goop. One yoni Facebook page advertises a 'Magic Wand Vaginal Tightening Stick' that promises to 'make you feel like a virgin again'. It doesn't list its ingredients, but I go to a different website that also sells yoni wands – Borneol, pearl powder, honeysuckle flower and terminal tree. It advises that the wand should be used daily for thirty seconds and used up to thirty times, and promises it will tighten your yoni, improve its elasticity and rid the yoni of bacterial vaginosis and odour. But wait – that's not enough! It will also help balance the vagina's pH, regulate your menstrual cycle, enhance sexual sensation, enhance lubrication, stimulate the female hormone to delay ageing AND climate toxins. Apart from all of this being pure baloney and possibly leading to other problems, it perpetuates the idea that vaginas are inherently dirty and need cleaning, which isn't true; they're self-cleaning. Amazon reviews reveal some of the results of using these scientifically baseless items. 'The product does tighten but it was very drying,' writes an American user. 'My boyfriend noticed I was very dry – that wasn't fun.' Another says, 'It did make me tighter but it also caused cramps and a slight loss of feeling. After 24 hours I had horrible itching and burning.' Unfortunately for one user, it wasn't only her that dealt with the discomfort. 'I tried to use this without letting [my boyfriend] know, but it hurt so bad when he peed after I had to tell him. I was mortified.' If a product makes you tight because it inflames the inside of your vagina as well as your partner's penis with an infection, is that really the tightness you were after?

Beyond yoni healing, there are plenty of advertisements for creams also promising to make you feel like a virgin again, including one that is literally called Virgin Again that I find advertised by a Pakistani shop on YouTube. The ingredients listed are all plants and crystal minerals. On Amazon, it says that the gel 'is especially dedicated to those partners who lose their interest in each other without knowing the cause. This solution gives a complete youthfulness and brings back the vagina into its original shape and enhances lovemaking desire in women.'

Such creams form the greater part of what Amazon offers me when I search 'vaginal tightening', but there's more. I'm also advertised an intimate skin-lightening cream for the body, bikini and sensitive areas that says it can be used on men, women and teenagers, promising to return a 'radiant youthful glow'.

Another space that often seems more interested in advertising tightness methods than in directing women to information about strengthening their pelvic floor muscles is the global vaginal rejuvenation market, which is estimated to be worth $5 billion by 2026, according to Global Market Insights. To put that into perspective, the breast augmentation market worldwide is only expected to reach $3.05 billion by 2027 as its popularity appears to be growing at a slower rate. North America enjoys the largest market share, which according to Grand View Research is down to the number of procedures available as well as the high disposable income of consumers – but Europe and the

Asia Pacific regions also form considerable slices of the pie chart. There are concerns among the medical community that some people are pursuing these surgeries needlessly and because of negative and patriarchal societal standards. In the UK, we know that between 2015 and 2016 more than 200 girls had a labiaplasty on the NHS, with 150 of them under fifteen years old – even though gynaecologists recommend the procedure should only be done on people who are over eighteen, when the body has finished developing and individuals are mature enough to take on such a surgery. The rise in labial reduction is universal (in the US, labiaplasties rose by over 217 per cent from 2012 to 2017) and the most common age group to get the procedure is twenty-five to thirty-four. In addition to cosmetic motives, there are clinical reasons to need such a surgery, such as irritation from over-large labia that prevent the wearing of tight clothes, psychological distress due to the labia being visible when wearing such clothing, or chronic urinary tract infection due to the pooling of sweat. But a GP told the *Evening Standard* that some girls overstate symptoms to get the NHS surgery and blame the rise on unrealistic images of vaginas in porn and social media. She told the newspaper: 'I'm seeing young girls around eleven, twelve, thirteen, thinking there's something wrong with their vulva – that they're the wrong shape, the wrong size, and really expressing almost disgust.' This is not helped by men online who share images of 'loose vaginas', which actually just show perfectly normal, larger labia than they may have seen in pornography.

That labiaplasty and labial trimming exist as cosmetic interventions for people who have no day-to-day problems with their labia, other than their self-esteem, is an indictment of how little we understand the labia, and testament to how long we have vilified anything about the female organ that might be considered 'big'. History features many butchering surgeons who would minimise labia and clitorises for fear they were making a woman's sexual appetite uncontrollable; now, it's surgeons profiting off beauty standards in which an idealised, 'virginal' vagina has small labia.

'Bullshit!' Dee Hartman declares as I tell her about Dr Seng Khoo's 'labial trimming' offering. She is an expert in pelvic floor therapy, with the majority of her twenty-seven years of experience dedicated to treating women with chronic vulvar pain and sexual dysfunction. 'Every hair on my body . . .' she starts to say, shivering at the thought and pulling out an illustration of the vulva and clitoris. In lots

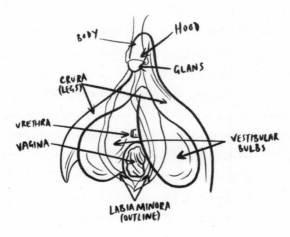

of medical images, we only really get to see the small glans – but really, the clitoris is far bigger.

'This is all part of the arousal network. We only really ever talk about the clitoris but the whole body of it is quite arousable. Blood flow comes to all of it just like it comes to all of the male; we get engorged.' She points towards the two pendulous bulbs either side. 'Vestibular bulbs also get full of blood and swell, they get more reactive to touch and they swell and put pressure on the vaginal canal. The labia are very sensual tissue. In most pictures you will just see the glans.'

She produces another set of illustrations, this time hand drawings from a physician in 1933, who documented a series of women's labia. 'The only thing normal about labia is diversity,' she says. 'And that's not just labia to labia, that's left to right.' She shakes her head. 'The thought that they get bigger with sex is . . . yeuuugh. Labia minora are filled with small blood vessels. If you trim them . . . you lose part of that arousal network.'

Writing for *The Conversation* in 2016, Gemma Sharp and Julie Mattiske discussed research they had conducted into the psychological outcomes of the procedure. 'We found women experienced significant improvements in satisfaction with their genital appearance from pre- to post-surgery. But we found no significant improvements in any other psychological domains, such as self-esteem and sexual confidence.' They also found that women who were more psychologically distressed – showing depression and anxiety symptoms in particular – or were currently in an intimate relationship were more likely to be dissatisfied after labiaplasty. This clashes with research finding that half of websites offering female genital cosmetic surgery promise enhanced sexual pleasure, with one claiming that 'sensation may even be enhanced because of the new nerve endings and removal of the tissue'. One of the top Google results, Esprit Cosmetic Surgeons, claims labiaplasty can make women 'feel open to new experiences', 'reduces pain during sex' and 'increases libido'. But none of these have scientific grounding. Dee is concerned that women seeking out these procedures to improve sexual sensations are probably not addressing the actual problem. 'Clitoral dehooding?' she asked, aghast. 'You can find the clitoris without dehooding. What exactly are you trying to solve here?'

Some of these pernicious views around what a vagina should look like – especially what a virginal or non-promiscuous vagina should look like – also affect the grotesque practice of female genital mutilation (FGM) around the world; there are over 200 million survivors today, with 100,000 of them living in the UK. When I was researching FGM, I came across an image of a vagina on Facebook of a woman with type 3 FGM, where the labia are sewn together to leave a tiny hole behind. The picture was so distant from what a vagina should look like that Facebook's moderation bots hadn't flagged it for nudity. It simply resembled the skin of an arm or thigh. It was only when you drew closer that you realised the pockmarks in the skin were an anus, vagina and urethra.

While not all FGM around the planet is undertaken to preserve a woman's chastity, a great deal of it is, and despite calls to ban the practice entirely by 2030, views on what a vagina should look like continue to thwart campaigners' and doctors' progress today. Dr Jasmine Abdulcadir, an FGM specialist doctor in Geneva, has seen victims from twenty-one different countries around the world pass through her clinic. She often carries out the practice of defibulation, the surgery that cuts through the scarred tissue to try to reconstruct a healthy vaginal opening. 'The closing of the genitals is imagined to be virginity,' she explains. 'So during defibulation, many of them who have even already suffered with severe complications are worried. They don't have a partner and they are afraid of not finding a husband because they aren't married.'

Erroneous beliefs around vaginal tightness also contribute to the second virginity test that exists, other than a hymen examination – the 'laxity' test, or 'two-finger' test. Zainab Husain, who works at the digital news organisation Soch, is one of the activists who has recently successfully petitioned the Lahore High Court to outlaw these virginity tests in rape examinations there.

'In Karachi, the biggest city in Pakistan, we have three medical legal departments. We went to the biggest of the three – Jinnah Hospital – and we literally just turned up, we got in touch with the woman running it. She was really suspicious with us, she had a police officer with us in this huge fancy office and she questioned us. We said that we'd just graduated, which we had done, and I think if we had been older she wouldn't have let us in. But we were twenty or twenty-one, really unassuming. She let us in to meet the medical legal officers, the people who write a report when you've been raped or assaulted. There were only three MLOs [medico-legal officers], now there are four. According to Pakistani law a woman has to be seen by a woman officer; it's illegal for her to be seen by a male. So, if you've been raped, you have to track one of these three officers in the seventy-two-hour time frame.

'When we got to the MLOs room, it was disgusting. Stark contrast to the boss's office. There was this huge sofa where everyone was sitting and reading. They didn't even have an examination table. They didn't have any place to store rape kits. When we interviewed them, they told us that they'd been taught at medical school that the laxity of the vagina would help them figure out if a woman was a virgin before she was raped. When we asked what connection her virginity had to do with her rape, they were just like, "Of course it has everything to do with it." They said that 50 per cent of the test was the two-finger virginity test, and 30 per cent was a chemical test.'

Zainab and her colleague produced two videos to address the appalling conditions, not only of the examination space but also of the inspection that young women had to undergo if they had been attacked, which provoked a public outcry. 'What relevance does it have whether she was a virgin or not?' Zainab asks me. 'We got a group of activists and journalists and psychologists and lawyers who've somehow been working on this issue with rape victims. The lawyers drafted a great argument with the Lahore High Court to ban the two-finger test and the hymen test.'

The court ruled the tests as unconstitutional, but now Zainab wants to make sure that this law is implemented and that medico-legal officers are trained, as well as judges and lawyers. 'We saw in court proceedings that judges ask medico-legal officers if the girl was a virgin or not – they know they're going to be asked this, which incentivises them to keep doing it.'

*

Other than labiaplasty, there is another surgery called vaginoplasty – an enormously wide-reaching term that covers a number of different procedures, surgical and non-surgical, but practically always refers to a narrowing of the vagina. You might have heard the term used in male-to-female gender reassignment surgery, when surgeons construct an entire vagina from scratch, but people with female genitalia can get vaginoplasties too to tighten what's already there. In surgery, 'extra' skin is removed from inside the vagina and the tissues beneath them are sutured tight. Non-surgical methods tighten the vagina through heat, either with radio frequency or with laser. A literature review from the *International Journal of Women's Health* in 2017 warned that 'they cannot be classified as aesthetic surgical interventions. Whereas accepted cosmetic/plastic surgery interventions such as breast augmentation or education are specifically performed to improve appearance and enhance self-confidence, this does not properly seem to be the case of vaginal rejuvenation procedures.' Vaginal tightening procedures are yet to win over the world's leading gynaecological bodies, who all recommend against it.

That hasn't stopped these procedures getting all over TV. There are at least three 'Real Housewives' who have had laser vaginal tightening – one on camera. On an episode of *Kocktails with Khloe*, Khloe Kardashian is shown discussing vaginal lasering procedures with TV plastic surgeon Dr Terry Dubrow, who adds, 'It works . . . it shrinks the inside and it basically . . . re-virginises you. It's like a face-lift of the vagina, sort of.' Viewed by millions, plastic surgery and aesthetic procedures featured on reality television have the power to instantly normalise procedures.

In a labiaplasty and vaginoplasty Facebook group I'm in, women are constantly talking about them. A number of the posts do point to an array of dissatisfied as well as satisfied customers. One asks if it's normal to experience painful orgasms after vaginoplasty; another says that their orgasms are so much better than before the surgery, but that they do hurt: 'I sit all day at work in agony.' Countless women say that their husbands don't complain or say anything, but that they are convinced they need tightening. One asks, 'This is probably a goofy question but . . . my cosmetic gyn takes the partner's girth into consideration for the vaginoplasty. How accurate do I need to be on it?' Only one person replies. 'Mine never asked. I had one consultation with a male plastic surgeon who said he could put me back to virgin status. The female plastic surgeon told me it would be two fingers wide – I was much more comfortable with the female doctor so I went with her.' What exactly 'virgin size' is, isn't elaborated on – needless to say, it doesn't exist.

One woman, an American called Sandy, tells me that it was the number of botched surgeries in the group that put her off invasive methods. Instead, she got vaginal lasering, which she'd seen featured on Jada Pinkett Smith's talk show *The Red Table*. Pinkett Smith says her vagina 'looks like a peach' and that it has improved her bladder function. The clinician holds up what looks like a vibrator but is in fact a tool used to laser the vagina, encouraging collagen production, which helps to improve elasticity and tone, as well as stimulating the creation of new blood vessels and nerves, which helps to produce lubrication. Sandy tells me that she's only had one treatment so far, but that she is already feeling the effects – her bladder control has improved. She adds: 'I also did this procedure for the tightening effect for an improved sexual experience and my partner says he can also tell a difference.' Some trials, however, are slowly debunking the efficacy of these offerings. In October 2021, Australian researchers shared their findings on a laser treatment being offered to menopausal women to rejuvenate the vagina. Eighty-five women were given either the laser treatment or a placebo, and while no serious side-effects were recorded in those who were treated, during the year follow-up there was no discernible improvement between the two groups. Simply put, the rejuvenation sold as repairing these women's sex lives and health completely failed in its objective.

One woman, however, was intent on getting a surgical intervention – and very much does believe in 'the virgin size'. Jay Shantal is a Christian life coach for single women, who grew up in Orlando, Florida, and is one of the few women to have made a YouTube video talking about her vaginoplasty experience. 'I grew up around a lot of drugs, violence, sex,' she tells me, 'and then God made a way.' She was a first-generation college student and by the time she was entering her early twenties she had started to consider celibacy. 'I felt less empowered by sex and more empowered by saving myself and the idea of saving myself. Now I help single women enjoy singleness.'

When she met her husband, she decided that she wanted to give him something she wished she had saved for him all along – her virginity. He too was celibate and also a virgin. 'When you start having sex when you're fourteen – by that point I was twenty-four, twenty-five. It had been almost eleven years. I don't think that I felt the same. I wanted my husband to have the experience that I wanted him to have. I wanted him to have the experience of going inside of me for the first time.' Earlier in our chat, Jay had said that she doesn't feel like she was safeguarded as much as she should have been when she was a teenager. 'Did you feel like you were giving yourself an experience that you wish life had granted you?' I asked her, and she immediately replied,

'Yes, I did. More women would love to make that change if they could. That fresh beginning. Taking back what was taken from them. We are the ones who bear the burden of "I can see that you've been active".' Who it was that Jay was imagining telling her this exactly was unclear.

You can't see or feel if a woman has a history of sexual activity or not. But that's not what we're taught. At school I can remember a girl who was called a 'bucket'. Online, incel forums call sexually active women roasties, because it's believed that their vulva looks like roast beef. Again, that is completely erroneous. But for Jay, that doesn't matter – in herself she truly believed that something wasn't right. 'My ex had a big penis. I knew that it wouldn't be the same after that. Even while having sex, I knew that my vagina was changing. When it would go inside – ouch! I wasn't doing that anymore.'

Jay decided to look into a popular laser treatment that she had seen advertised and had a consultation with an aesthetic gynaecologist. I asked her if he told her that she looked like her vagina had borne some kind of sexual use or trauma. 'He didn't say I looked wider,' she said. 'He was like, this is something that you want to do. He said there was room for improvement but he didn't say that it was stretched out.' I asked her if any of her former partners had also given her any cause for concern. She pauses for a moment and thinks. 'In the midst of having sex I never heard any complaints but I think when I became celibate I got really fixated on a phys-ical manifestation of celibacy and a rebirth and looking at myself. And feeling some level of guilt about my sexual past, and [wanting to] right my wrongs. I had to go through my own healing process to make sure I wasn't trying to remedy something but get down to the more emotional side of it.'

Her husband-to-be completely supported her, but did ask questions about her sexual past to try to understand her thought process. She says he was very understanding and gentle, and that she's actually had a number of women message her who are struggling with similar attempts to reconcile a sexual past with a celibate present and married future. 'This is nothing I wanted to talk about online; I wanted to keep it private like everyone else. But when I did research I didn't see any black women talking about it. I saw a doctor's interview about it, that's it. No woman was coming out and saying that they had had a vaginoplasty. Or saying that they don't feel the same down there. I wanted to make that change.' Happy with her results, as well as the sex she and her husband enjoyed on her wedding night, Jay feels like she has succeeded in her mission. I asked if any of the clients that she life coaches had also considered a vaginoplasty after her video. They hadn't. I also asked her if, before even going to a surgeon in the first place, she'd thought about going to see a doctor in case there were exercises or a health issue at play that she could resolve to get 'tighter'. She said no and was surprised – as if that wasn't really an option.

'Could she have had muscle issues? Might Kegel exercise have worked?' asks Dr Lincoln, who continues: 'They might have, they might not have. The kind of surgery that she had – the risks are high. If there's over-tightening there can be scarring, there can be dyspareunia. What scares me is that in one of the medical journals there's always an ad that says you can take on a course in vaginal rejuvenation. If you say that you're experienced in offering these procedures and your explanation is "I did a weekend course and I'm certified", that worries me. There's a reason we do thousands of medical procedures before we're considered competent enough to do them. But if you're a layperson, it can be really hard to work this out. They have a nice office, nice furniture. They say they're certified to do it – why wouldn't it be safe?'

*

That GripTok and Kegel trends have become so viral on TikTok, and that so many young women seem increasingly interested in tightening methods, speaks to how younger age demographics are becoming increasingly aware of the pressure of vaginal tightness without necessarily experiencing an improvement in understanding of vaginal health. While some of this kind of content – as well as the advertising that surrounds vaginal rejuvenation – seems to be targeted at any woman whatsoever, it's undeniable that a great deal of it is aimed at women who have had children. Online, I soon find a doctor in the North West of England who has written a blog about it. 'Following childbirth,' he explains, 'the vagina does not return to its initial position and therefore the stimulation of the vaginal walls during sexual intercourse decreases.' He goes on to say that childbirth means that the vagina remains wider, especially if the woman is over thirty-five, and that 'even a planned C-section is not absolute protection', adding that 'during pregnancy the woman's hormones reduce the muscle tone, the pregnant uterus presses on the vagina and ligaments and muscles cause vaginal and uterine prolapse of different severity'. He doesn't once recommend pelvic floor therapy; instead, he recommends non-surgical vaginal rejuvenation that will last up to two years – which he incidentally performs himself.

It is true that childbirth can alter the vagina in different ways, but the obsession with returning to pre-birth shape, rather than encouraging a) pelvic floor therapy that will improve function across your bladder and rectum too and b) the absence of affirmation that a body is allowed to change after childbirth, paints a dismal picture for women, who, inundated by cultural output that fetishises tight vaginas, see themselves as inferior. Some women have reported that they have been subjected to a 'husband stitch' – an additional stitch during repair from a tear or episiotomy, which has no approved medical use – by doctors without their consent; though data on this is scant, there are many appalling anecdotal reports.

In an article for Healthline in 2018, one woman explains that she had years of painful sex after delivering her first child. Years later at a pap smear, a healthcare provider told her that something wasn't right, and that it looked like the doctor had given the supposed husband stitch without her consent. On Reddit, I quickly find a woman who, fifteen years after discovering the husband stitch had been done to her, felt the need to share her story. 'My husband said there was a wide ridge of scar tissue there,' she explains, 'and after more intense self-exploration, I realised that the intern had "stitched me up nice and tight" alright, by sewing closed a half-inch or more of my vaginal opening just above my perineum.' She saw another doctor who confirmed that this had happened and assured her that a second delivery would help fix the damage that had been done. That doctor was happily correct – and she has been able to have pain-free sex ever since. 'Ironically, the pain from the stitching seriously impeded my, and my husband's, sex lives for more than two years.

Thankfully, the husband stitch seems to be a relic of the past; if a minority of doctors are continuing to practise it, it serves as yet another reason to improve pelvic floor training and support to medical staff. This would certainly help strengthen new mothers battling with possible sexual dysfunction; a 2020 study published in the *Sexual Medicine* journal found that third- and fourth-degree tears were strongly associated with postpartum sexual dysfunction, while episiotomy did not adversely affect sexual function. When women give birth, their oestrogen plummets to make way for prolactin, a hormone that aids breastfeeding, and oxytocin, the bonding hormone that helps them look after their baby; the result is a completely natural, physiological loss of libido. In the Facebook support group I am in for vaginoplasty and labiaplasty, a high number of the women describe a loss of sexual pleasure after childbirth. The idea that the problem might be solved by further surgery and trauma to the area – a labiaplasty that literally removes some of the arousal network, or procedures such as clitoral dehooding – seem woefully misguided.

In France, the government subsidises *la rééducation périnéale* – perineal re-education – for all new mothers. In an essay for *Slate* in 2012, American Claire Lundberg described her experience of being prescribed ten to twenty sessions of it in Paris. From her perspective, she describes France as a country where 'everyone wants you to be able to have sex with your husband again as soon as possible' before he 'finds a mistress', as well as ensuring you can easily and safely have another child. Whatever the reasoning, she feels much better after it. Even enlightened France also boasts its own industry of vaginal rejuvenation – but at least women of all socioeconomic backgrounds can access medical support before they reach out for Dr Google.

*

How we unlearn the tightness and youthfulness myth is tricky, and unfortunately not helped by men on the internet. After Pornhub removed all of its unverified content in 2020 – which eradicated an enormous number of its dubious '18+' teen videos – one internet user reacted with: 'Pornhub literally took everything off their site. It's all big fake tits and loose vaginas now.' 'Tight vagina' is not only how men label pornographic content they encounter online, it is also how women advertise themselves on platforms such as OnlyFans.

Similar to the lust for hymeneal blood, the desire to penetrate a tight vagina has encouraged women to create and recreate their own anatomy to cater for the male experience. That such myths around the penis and male virginity don't exist is telling. In the subreddit r/badwomensanatomy, a vibrant resource that mocks sexual misinformation on the internet, one user posts pictures of two sausages. The first is large, thick, like a chorizo. 'The penis of a virgin,' it says. 'Penis is still large and healthy. It hasn't been crushed inside dozens of vaginas and will one day make the right woman a very happy wife.' Next to it is a long, thin Peperami. 'The penis of a man who has had multiple sexual partners. Penis has shrivelled down to less than 1/3 of its original size due to vaginal pressure and will no longer be able to pleasure any woman.' The post has received thousands of upvotes. 'This isn't accurate,' replies a user called frogglesmash, 'repeated intercourse actually makes the penis larger, spongy, and incapable of erections. This is due to becoming waterlogged with vaginal fluid.' The post was shared in an incel forum, whose members completely missed the irony of the post. But the female users kept liking and commenting.

'Vaginal Pressure would be a great band name,' replied one of them. I agree.

4

The Penetration Myth

When Quinn Birkholz had sex for the first time, they turned to their partner and smiled. 'I can't believe I've finally done it!' they exclaimed. But their excitement was quickly expunged when Quinn's partner responded with, 'No, you didn't?'

What Quinn had just experienced was intense, especially because both of them had climaxed, but the reason that their partner decided to relegate Quinn's experience to being somehow 'less' was because no penetration had been involved, i.e. anal sex. Years later, Quinn is now an active YouTube sex educator talking freely about homosexual experiences and their realisation that they are non-binary.

'We inherit ideas around virginity in the queer community. Top and bottom; masculine and feminine; passive and active; penetrator and the penetrated. It is absurd.'

Top and bottom are useless labels for Quinn, but they're often used in gay dating spaces, especially Grindr. 'I don't feel like I need to categorise it. By someone asking that question, it means that there's an importance on penetrative sex for them. There's this new label, "sides", for people who don't want these labels. A side is a man who doesn't do anal. It's not a label I use to define myself, but it's really interesting.'

Sides could be onto something. In the *Journal of Sexual Medicine*, researchers from Indiana University and George Mason University surveyed nearly 25,000 gay and bisexual men and found that the most commonly reported behaviour included kissing followed by oral sex (73 per cent) and partnered masturbation (64 per cent). Less than half of the participants reported anal sex – disputing the widely held notion that that is what most gay men do in bed. But it is obvious that LGBTQIA sexualities have taken on heteronormative gender scripts; a study from the *Journal of Adolescent Health* in 2007 found that while 99.5 per cent of students thought vaginal intercourse was sex, only 81 per cent thought penile-anal contact was sex and just 40 per cent thought oral-genital contact was sex. That world view doesn't leave much room for qualifying gay sex.

Quinn has seen this have a very real influence on the power and gender dynamics that are applied to gay sex, which should be seen as far more fluid. 'You can have a very active person being penetrated – we call that a power bottom. You can have someone dominant and be penetrated. You can have someone who is masculine being penetrated AND submissive. If you connect the dots, there's a million different combinations. These labels are so silly and they perpetuate these same harmful ideas around virginity. I wish I'd been taught that anal sex isn't something I'm going to have to do to have a happy life.'

The same goes for lesbian experiences. One woman told me she'd got into an argument with a man once because, while he conceded that anal sex qualified as virginity loss for men, strap-on sex or any kind of sex at all wouldn't qualify as virginity loss for women. 'It's symptomatic of how mainstream conceptions of sex focus hard on penises and define sex by penises. If it doesn't involve a penis then it's foreplay and not sex. Eventually I was able to argue that I was sexually experienced given that I've had a threesome in a BDSM club. He still insisted that I was a virgin though, just a sexually experienced one.' She said that, for her, cinema was especially damaging, with its absence of lesbian leads or female leads undefined by their relationship to a male partner. 'Gay guys don't tend to have as much angst over this,' she clarifies, 'but lesbians tend to sleep with guys because the social pressure to do so is enormous. Women are defined by the relationships we have with men.'

It's not just relationships: it's sex. One study found that 68 per cent of women said it counts as sex when a partner gives them oral sex, but only 33 per cent of men said it counts when they give a partner oral sex. Durex found that 30 per cent of men believe vaginal penetration is the best way to make a woman orgasm, whereas over half the women they surveyed said it was clitoral stimulation. This focus on penetration is costing women orgasms; psychologist Laurie

Mintz's anonymous polling of her students over the years revealed to her that 55 per cent of men say that they usually reach orgasm during first-time hookup sex. Guess what the number is for women. Higher? Lower? It's over ten times lower, at just 4 per cent.

A study in 2020 found that it takes women on average 13.46 minutes from the beginning of arousal to orgasm; compare that to another study that found the average penetrative sex session length was 5.4 minutes. If sex doesn't make room for female pleasure experiences, it isn't equitable. We don't have language on our side here; as Kate Lister observes in *A Curious History of Sex*, there are 2,500 slang words for the penis in the encyclopaedia of profanity, *Roger's Profanisaurus*, compared to simply five for the clitoris. The word vagina comes from the Latin for sword sheath; in other words, the vagina is a receptacle, or holder for the penis. It exists to serve the sword. Even the analogy of sex as first, second and third base leads to the last base, holy grail of the penis. Clit stuff is demoted to mere 'foreplay', a word that suggests non-penetrative activity comes *before* sex, as opposed to it being sex itself, or indeed coming during and after penetrative intercourse.

But this is not inclusive of the LGBTQIA community, or women. In April 2021 researchers from the Indiana University School of Medicine released a new vocabulary to help women verbalise what it is they often do in bed – essentially manoeuvring their bodies during penetration so that it becomes less penis-focused, specifying actions such as rocking the clitoris against their partner, or pairing self-touch with penetration. Only two-decades-old research has shown us that the enormous, nerve-ending-filled clitoral structure swells around the walls of the vagina, proving the importance of its role in penetration. Penetration will always be a feature of sex, but it is just one – in a world where there is a plethora of tools and techniques at hand. What it doesn't have to do is reinforce tired old gender dynamics, and heteronormativity. An insistence that 'proper' sex must be penetrative is ableist too, diminishing the many varied ways in which those with disabilities enjoy sex and intimacy. The non-disabled, in fact, have a lot to learn from the exploration of erogenous zones, which many disabled people value as highly fulfilling sexual expression.

This chapter is going to take aim at the penetration myth: the notion that certain people give while others take, that some people initiate while others remain coy, that transformative sex is penetrative and starts and ends with a penis. This is one of the most damaging sex myths around today and has a direct impact on our sex lives. It also perpetuates many of the ideas we have about virginity: that women must let blood when they are penetrated for the first time, that their bodies show the markings of such activity, and that it is penetration which transforms their social status from child to woman, from virgin to wife or slut.

This is the myth that I, and those I grew up with, so poorly understood. And it is what led to one of the unhappiest periods of my life.

*

Across your social circles – your family, friends, colleagues and acquaintances – there will be at least one woman who has never been able to have sex. Every time she tries, it feels like her sexual partner is stabbing her insides with a dagger. The pain is not a dull, throbbing ache that you might be able to tolerate through gritted teeth, and there is no sense of something hard yet fleshlike entering you – it's a switchblade slicing towards your cervix. Your whole body convulses and you're left bruised from what could be many failed attempts at entry, even when you want to have sex with every will in the world. The condition has a name and in the UK it affects one in 500 women. It is one of the most common female sexual disorders, and yet you've probably never heard of it.

I had not heard of it as I began to flirt online with a twenty-seven-year-old man I met in a music shop. I was seventeen, and had only ever really kissed before. Not only had no one else really been *down there* – *I* hadn't been down there either. I hadn't been told about the research that shows masturbation has health benefits, and that masturbation in adolescence leads to more positive self-image and better sex lives in adulthood. I was, instead, wholly disinterested. I'd tried and failed to use tampons; they hurt, and when I was told that I'd be able to use them 'after I had sex', I assumed that's because sex somehow opened you up, a *penis* opened you up. Pleasure had never been described to me as something I might try to bring about myself – a likely consequence of a Catholic upbringing, stigma around female masturbation and the way that more experienced male partners were validated at school. I had understood I needed someone to show me the ropes. It was unthinkable I could show *myself* the ropes; in order to become a woman, and have sex, and maybe even orgasm, I had assumed I would need a man. To think any of these could have been achieved without the presence of a penis would have been anathema to me, and it certainly wouldn't have made me feel like I could be taken seriously by my peers, the majority of whom were now months, even years, ahead of me in entering sexual maturity. On top of all this, I'd heard all the stories at school about hymens and blood, condoms and penises of various sizes. Everything about the language of sex felt threatening and aggressive – excitingly so, but also scarily so. The older I got, the less likely it seemed that this suitor might be a high school boyfriend, and in that vacuum, the music shop man appeared.

A survey published in 2021 showed that a high proportion of British women and men are completely incapable of labelling all the parts of the vulva. Over half couldn't correctly identify that women have three holes and, regardless of their gender, half of Britons couldn't identify the urethra and 37 per cent mislabelled the clitoris. This builds on what other researchers have found. A US study revealed that 46 per cent of women surveyed couldn't point out the cervix, and a quarter didn't know where their vagina was. This was me; I'd have struggled to identify anything other than the womb and fallopian tubes on a diagram, because that's all I learnt in biology. I might have been about to turn eighteen, but as the Natsal survey described at the beginning of this book, I was a long way from being their definition of 'sexually competent'.

I didn't grow up in a prudish house, but I did have a lot of pressure on me to do well at school and focus on my studies. Boys were, generally speaking, a no-go. All I ever felt when I kissed someone, apart from affection, was extreme guilt. I had to lie to my parents when I was out seeing someone to avoid scrutiny. But this twenty-seven-year-old man was involved in a ruse too. He never wanted to meet in public, something I realise now showed how disturbingly clear our age difference was to him. All I saw was someone experienced. But in the darkness of his bedroom, dotted with guitars and superhero paraphernalia, I slowly recognised that I was not in the company of a suave, capable adult. Hours later, at the moment of truth, he started going through all of his drawers, one after the other, slamming them shut percussively as he tried the next one, then the next one. 'I don't have any condoms,' he said. 'It's okay – I'll pull out.'

I jolted. That wasn't part of the plan. Didn't all men have condoms? I was scared – too scared to have sex, too scared not to give him what he wanted and also too scared to walk out of his house having failed to achieve what I'd set out to do. I felt embarrassed. What happened next, I learned only months later, was that we didn't actually have sex at all.

Because every time he tried, pain would zap through me, and my body would curl up in agony.

Was that it? I thought. I concluded that sex was dismally painful and mainly about what a man wanted to do in or on you. A few months later I was in a relationship at university with someone I was completely devoted to, and it was after failed attempts with him that he told me, as sensitively as you can tell someone, that I had in fact not lost my virginity and that maybe I should see a doctor.

While everyone else in my halls was regaling one another with tales of first-term debauchery, I laughed conspiratorially and never let on about the sexual problems I was having, nor that I spent that whole first term in countless GP appointments, sitting sheepishly in the surgery waiting room hoping nobody would recognise me and ask me what I was doing there. It is the first time in my life I've really understood what 'taboo' meant. When I went in and explained what had happened, the male GP asked if I had ever been sexually abused, to which I shook my head. Then he asked me to take my knickers off and lie down on the examination table. I felt like something must be very wrong with me. He attempted to look inside, but as I raised my buttocks, my thighs jammed shut. He shook his head. 'I'm not going to be able to get a speculum in to look,' he said, and I felt like a failure, again. He took a swab, which hurt, then told me to wait for results.

Once he'd ruled out an infection, I was still back and forth at the surgery, searching helplessly for a way to stop the pain. The GP prescribed me lidocaine, a local anaesthetic cream. As sensitive as my boyfriend was, all the toing and froing of doctor's appointments and failed sex attempts had launched me into depression. The doctor hadn't advised I try other kinds of sex, or have a break from sex for a while; he said to keep trying, which I was later informed was one of the worst things someone could have told me to do, never mind a medical professional. Night after night, I was essentially self-harming in an attempt to cure myself. I became convinced I would not only lose my boyfriend's interest, but never gain the interest of anyone else because something about me was defective. Maybe I'd never be able to have sex, and that meant I would never be able to have children. While all my friends were preoccupied with pre-drinks and nights out, I was losing sleep and, gradually, my mind over my fertility and any future prospect of love.

The lidocaine, which I needed my boyfriend's help to apply because I *still* didn't understand my own anatomy, didn't work. From studies I've read, I've seen that this prescription isn't unusual, and seems to have even helped some people, but it didn't help me. What was really going on was psychological, spasming my entire pelvic floor, and felt totally out of my control. At the end of my tether, I went back to the surgery and this time asked for a second opinion. I was given a female GP, who within seconds said, 'You've got vaginismus.' She immediately reassured me of how common it was and that near my university there was actually an excellent psychosexual clinic where I would be able to get treatment in the form of dilators and psychological therapy. She said she would refer me. And maybe it was finally having a name on it – finally learning and being able to tell my boyfriend that it was curable – but within a couple of months, before the referral letter ever came, one day, sex simply just happened. My muscles obeyed me, and I was fine. And I've never had a problem having sex since.

Vaginismus is oddly christened – it sort of means 'the condition of being a vagina' and was given that name back in 1862 when it was first mentioned during an address at the Obstetrical Society of London. It is defined as the involuntary spasming of the pelvic floor when penetration is attempted. This doesn't have to be by a penis – it could be a speculum for a cervical smear, a tampon, a sex toy, anything. Many have experiences like mine: a failed tampon or sex toy insertion, and then failed first-time sex. Then the second. Then the third. There's a wall and no matter what you try, nothing eases it; the pain becomes so sharp and all-consuming that even the thought of trying it again launches some women into panic attacks. 'There is probably an older woman in your life who almost certainly never had children because they have vaginismus,' one gynaecologist said to me. Let that thought percolate. This pain condition is so widespread that not only could there be a woman in your life quietly coping with it – there could be women whose ability to have children has been dictated by it. It destroys relationships, it destroys families and it destroys mental wellbeing; the same gynaecologist told me that 'it destroys lives'.

Vaginismus is completely curable, often through physical and psychological therapy, but the taboo and lack of awareness mean that many go months and years waiting for a diagnosis, never mind a cure. I know this because between my journalism and my personal life, I've encountered countless women with this condition. In a scheme I am involved in, out of thirty people, two of them have messaged me about vaginismus, having had no idea that I had it too; that's one in ten. One of them is sat on long waiting lists in Scotland for psychosexual therapy, and the other has even debated moving to London and going private because she is struggling to find psychosexual therapy support where she lives.

Vaginismus is one of an array of sexual pain disorders that affect women. One in thirteen women in Britain experience pain during sex, but few openly discuss it, possibly because many are told it is normal for sex to hurt, so it's not a medical issue – as opposed to *it is normal for sex to hurt if a number of criteria, including your own comfort, have not been met.* It is astonishing that people – including some members of the medical community – can believe painful sex is normal for women, while simultaneously declining to administer anaesthetic for procedures such as inserting the coil, which is pushed through the cervix. Sex is supposed to hurt, but an IUD insertion isn't? The nuanced reality of women's actual experience is often ignored or poorly diagnosed, making for a confusing maze of acceptable and unacceptable pain. The revelation that nothing should hurt seems to have gone over some people's heads. But my friends languishing on waiting lists and the doctors misdiagnosing sexual pain disorders are surrounded by systems that are not stepping in to support or re-educate them.

Sexual health and psychosexual support in the UK have gone through several years of disinvestment; the King's Fund found that budget cuts of more than 20 per cent to genitourinary medicine (GUM) services in some parts of the country have led to clinic closures and staffing cuts. Clinical commissioning groups have stated that they have difficulty delivering seamless care in the area of psychosexual counselling; in layman's terms, that means the nuanced physical and psychological therapy needed for conditions such as vaginismus is rarely integrated. In 2015, there were cuts of £200 million to Public Health England and a 40 per cent reduction in the spending of local authorities, who run these services. I suspect that my friends are not the only ones sitting on waiting lists.

Other vaginismus sufferers I have interviewed have shared with me that they too felt that men were the agents of sex, and that engaging in penetrative sex was the only way to maintain men's interest. After I made a film about vaginismus for the BBC, a young woman called Elle Jane wrote about her three-year battle with different doctors and therapists in the UK and abroad, desperately trying to find out why sex was so painful that she couldn't experience any kind of penetration with her then boyfriend, Alex. After various diagnoses of vaginismus and a perineal tear later, as well as psychological therapy and an operation, she was eventually able to have sex with him. But those years of crushing disappointment took a toll. In her blog, she wrote: 'For three years, I had people telling me that they couldn't do it if they were Alex, that they would definitely cheat, [and] that he probably was. They were unaware of how often I told Alex to go sleep with other people. I thought about breaking up, because if I couldn't have sex, then I couldn't give him children one day. Some people also told him that he should break up [with me], because sex is a huge part of a relationship.'

Nearly one in ten British women experience pain during sex. While vaginismus is only one such pain disorder among women, it is one of the most common, and its inclusion in this book is vital because it is part of the first-time sex experiences of millions of women around the globe. Studies have tied it to virginity anxiety, as well as fear of sex and male sexual power, especially if you've lived somewhere where you've been taught to value female virginity and male sexual power above your own. You would think that a sex-obsessed world would have a vested interest in eradicating vaginismus. But a Cochrane review into clinical interventions for vaginismus only found 'five poor to moderate quality studies'. It adds that these trials only looked at physical therapies such as the use of dilators, completely ignoring the role of psychological therapy in treating what is widely considered to be a psychosexual disorder.

And when studies or doctors say 'clinicians aren't trained to treat it', they aren't joking. An American woman told me that the first two gynaecologists she saw said, 'Are you sure that you have a vagina?' and 'I feel really sorry for your ex-boyfriend,' after she explained the problems she was experiencing. Countless women are asked by doctors, 'Have you tried having a glass of wine first?' or 'Are you sure that you like your partner enough?' In other parts of the world, the picture for vaginismus sufferers looks even more dismal. Tunisian doctors described vaginismus in a 2019 paper as 'one of the most frequent causes of non-consummation of marriage, and of infertility, in Arab-Muslim societies'. Dr Sandrine Atallah, a well-known sexologist in Beirut, has had patients come to her after they were told by doctors they'd be put under anaesthesia while their husband had sex with them. 'I had another patient's doctor explain that he would do a hymenectomy [surgical removal of the hymen] and vagina enlargement, and so he put her under anaesthetic. When she woke up, she had a speculum between her legs. He told her, "Look, you have this between your legs, you're cured." She was so traumatised.'

Doctors who are in the know are begging for extra training and research. Dr Leila Frodsham, a consultant with the Royal College of Obstetricians and Gynaecologists, told me that in research she conducted, 100 per cent of medical students and 98 per cent of gynaecologists wanted more training in sexual dysfunction – and only 13 per cent of gynaecologists thought their training had been adequate. If that's how well-trained gynaecologists feel in this area, imagine how underprepared a GP must be – the first healthcare professional a woman is likely to meet on their diagnosis journey.

I will always be left wondering why I developed vaginismus, but in between the pain of tampons, the terror of what I thought would be my first sexual experience and the whole narrative I bought into that I was passive and not active in sex lie many ideas that I am certain a good sex education would have erased. What if it had occurred to my male GP that maybe, for a short while at least, my boyfriend and I might wish to forgo penetrative sex to best ensure my recovery? Researchers note that young people want to be talked to about non-penetrative sex, and my own journalism has suggested that there is an unthinkable number of women out there who still don't know vaginismus is a condition, with a name and with a cure. Let's talk about it – and let's treat it.

*

In order to truly debunk the penetration myth, there needs to be an ongoing story throughout people's sexual journeys; we need to reframe first-time sex as folding into a set of experiences, rather than one single moment.

This is something Frank agrees with, an American who claims he has slept with 181 virgins, arranged mainly through word of mouth. From school to college and now his working life, his supply of 'clients' has dried up slightly – that's what he calls them, even though there's no financial transaction involved in the service he provides. 'It's definitely decreased,' he tells me, now entering his mid-thirties. 'In the twelve years since college I've had just a little over thirty. About ten or twelve of them have been the younger siblings of previous clients.'

Frank found me through Reddit's intricate web of virginity forums, which he monitors when he has the time to see if there's anyone who needs help. One of Frank's hobbies, on top of his busy professional life and passion for sailing, is helping women have first-time sex. He does not divulge a kink for it, if he has one; when I ask him why he does it, he tells me: 'I like knowing there's one guy who's treated them well. There's a lot of guys that treat women like shit.'

He has given women their first sexual experiences across many of the twenty-three different countries he has lived in, but mainly in the United States. The 'programme' he has developed takes girls through foreplay and orgasm before they get to any kind of interaction with *his* body, then penetrative sex, different positions and then anything else they might want to try out. 'That's what I call the elective programme, if they want to explore kinks, restraints, subbing or domming, anal sex.' The first meeting is important; there's no touching and it's only considered completed if the girl is comfortable with seeing him naked, as well as being naked around him. One girl took thirty-seven meetings to take her clothes off. 'I've had girls who are nervous, fearful, especially if they've been indoctrinated to fear sex or to believe enjoying sex makes them a slut or whore.' He makes it clear that they should not expect a relationship with him before he agrees to offer the programme, and has dated both virgins and non-virgins in and around his 'teaching'.

That the first moment of penetrative sex might be seen as a *part* of sex rather than the *focus* of sex is something Frank is passionate about, hence why it comes halfway through his 'Introduction to Sex 101' curriculum. This is representative of the varied nature of sexual experiences, and conveys that penis-in-vagina (PIV) isn't the be-all and end-all that virginity-loss narratives purport it to be. When I ask Frank about how many of his clients would see virginity as a social construct, he tells me: 'Most of my clients are middle of the road. Its dismissal as a social construct to a certain degree reflects one's general ideas about sexuality.' He pauses. 'I wonder how many women who have had a traumatic experience would reflect on virginity as a social construct.' Frank can recall many clients with unhappy sexual histories. 'As someone who has been with partners who only had negative experiences, that is a steep mountain, disarming those negative associations.' He once had a girlfriend who had several sexual partners without ever experiencing an orgasm. 'The first time she had an orgasm, she locked herself in the bathroom because she didn't understand what had happened. I had to assure her it was okay.'

You might have some moral concerns informed by your own world view about Frank's self-appointed mission, but the experiences that he shares with women aren't only pleasure-informed, but trauma-informed. When we step into sexual scenarios with new people, we often don't communicate our sexual anxieties or problems. The penetration myth often leads to painful and pleasureless sex – a traumatic experience that leaves us feeling that sex has been inequitable and harmful. This affects us far beyond our sex lives. Dysfunction and poor mental and physical health often go hand in hand, causing each other to the point where it can often be hard to work out which started the other.

De-emphasising penetrative experiences with partners, and taking everything more slowly, will hugely benefit women and make sex healthier and fairer. It might have saved me from vaginismus, and my peers from other trauma too. A school friend of mine, who we'll call Katherine to preserve her privacy, sympathises with what Frank says. Aged seventeen, our friendship group was increasingly having first-time, second-time and many-time penetrative sex. She felt late to the party, as if she wasn't a proper woman yet – and as if her relationship wasn't a proper relationship, either. There was an unspoken idea floating around that you weren't truly serious with someone unless you'd had sex – as if, without it, your relationship couldn't qualify as an adult one. She was in a long-term relationship and had 'waited', like everyone told you to. She spontaneously decided, one day in her bedroom, that they would do it

– no prior communication necessary. He willingly went along with the unexpected permission, and entered her. She experienced what she describes as 'absolute pain' and didn't even know that he had penetrated her, because the pain obliterated any other possible sensation. The next day, he rang and announced that he had told his best friend. 'Told him what?' she asked. 'That we had sex,' he replied, a little deflated at her response. She said to me, '*I was thinking, phew, okay, I guess he's counting it then.*'

He counted it because he penetrated her, and he orgasmed. She didn't. And it was only a whole relationship and seven sexual partners later that she would orgasm, for the very first time, eight years later. Couldn't our schools and universities better prepare us before it gets to that stage? Why are we still seeing orgasms and painless sex as a sex issue? It is a health issue; a wellbeing issue; an equity issue too.

5

The Virility Myth

Originally, the 'shag list' was supposed to be ironic. Ben, Hildon and their housemates had written the names of conquests on their fridge's whiteboard, the nucleus of their daily life. Every time they needed milk, or butter, or a beer, they'd see where they ranked; more names meant more prestige. Given that two of the housemates were in long-term relationships, the shag list was never intended to pit the men against each other. It was supposed to be harmless fun, a small way to memorialise the hedonism of student life.

But that's not how those who visited their house saw it. When mates came over, their eyes would focus on Ben and Hildon's names as the two firmly single men of the house. This was where action was to be had – a real competition. The checking of the whiteboard every time friends came round became ritualised. Ben hated it, and repeatedly wiped the list off. But whenever they came round, it would be there again.

'I'd come back the next morning from dates and the questions were never "was she nice?" or "did she have good chat?"' Ben explains, having graduated a few years ago now. 'It was more along the lines of "was she fit?" Otherwise, the shag didn't count.'

Ben would try to avoid answering questions, uncomfortable with the idea that dates were being scrutinised and, if deemed worthy, reduced to names on a whiteboard. Hildon, mocked by his blank list every time he needed to eat something, eventually called a girl from home and invited her to stay for the weekend, just so he could say that he had slept with someone. He ignored her nearly the entire time she was there. 'He acted like he was ashamed of her,' said Ben.

Ben says now that he didn't mind being the butt of jokes; he was confident that his were funnier anyway, and didn't degrade anyone in the process either. When they left the house, the whiteboard was presumably wiped clean for one last time, and the shag list was never updated again. 'The message should be clear – attributing sex to masculine success is extremely unhealthy. It didn't make me feel any better about myself. I know from speaking to Hildon, who's also in a relationship [now], that he was fully aware too and admitted to being embarrassed about it. So, I guess, that's growth?'

*

Come on, be a man. Grow a pair, don't be a pussy, and get laid. Go hard or go home. I heard all of these masculinising refrains growing up, but especially at university, where I was thrust from the cattiness of an all-girls' school into the far more rabid environment of my student halls.

I met many sensitive, intelligent men at Durham, but I met plenty of insensitive, intelligent men there too. In the UK, we both celebrate and criticise our lad subculture. But at university it didn't feel like a subculture at all. It felt like *the* culture. As heterosexual women, my friends and I would have to operate in its orbit, sometimes mimicking it, sometimes hiding from it.

Wherever you live, there is an equivalent social structure that young men participate in. The British lad is the American bro frat boy. If you feel this doesn't apply to you, that is hopefully because you grew up in an environment where you were exposed to healthy ideas around masculinity. You may have had additional life experiences and identities such as being part of a queer community, which have allowed you to escape this myopic worldview. But many men feel like they're stratified into two groups: men who can't get any, and men who can. Just like Ben's student house, whether you want to be part of it or not makes little difference. Visions of virile assertiveness are considered the masculine ideal – and either you successfully perform that ideal, or you fail. As one young man tells me, 'We are taught to fuck without feeling.'

Where women have long been harmed by the virginity myth, in which sexual *in*experience increases their desirability, men have been harmed by the opposite idea – that sexual *experience*, prowess and success improves their status: the virility myth. Not only is sexual activity a positive, it's what you need to actively qualify as a man. Deriving from the Latin word *vir*, meaning 'man', virility serves as a byword for masculinity; sexual success is very literally written into our definition of male identity.

In order to achieve sexual success, mass media makes men feel that they must perform certain behaviours or obtain characteristics that we are socially conditioned to think of as masculine – gains at the gym, a strong jaw and a well-paid job. At Durham, that also included downing the most pints. While most heterosexual women would say that many things other than looks and power can make a man attractive, dating reveals uncomfortable truths that reinforce these gender scripts. As early as the 1930s, American women wanted their husbands to be more sexually experienced than them. Across three studies, Lauri Jensen-Campbell and her colleagues found that women *do* go for 'dominant men', but crucially, not dominance alone; they go for dominance *with* pro-social behaviours such as being agreeable or helping others. A survey of 7,000 Australian online dating users found that women aged eighteen to twenty-five placed a significant weight on age, education, intelligence, income, trust and emotional connection, in contrast to men of the same age group, who assigned higher priority to attractiveness and physical build in female partners. All the older respondents cared less about aesthetics than younger ones, so while looks aren't everything for women, there remain many factors that influence a power dynamic – such as an older age, higher intelligence or financial stability – that would thwart younger, financially unstable male suitors. A number of small surveys by dating sites consistently find that straight men are more likely to be open to date unemployed partners than the other way around.

The virility myth, and the fact that men and women continue to buy into it, is colliding with a world where social dynamics are in dramatic flux. Global unemployment is increasing, and just before the pandemic hit, trends were suggesting that the number of men who hadn't had sex in the past year had increased threefold; it is likely that spending longer periods of time in education and living with your parents is having an impact on young men's ability to perform virility. Women entering the workplace means that not only are the 'dominance' stakes often higher, but that women no longer rely on the institution of marriage to be economically stable. Being pickier is something that dating apps encourage, which we need to take seriously given that 32 per cent of relationships started between 2015 and 2019 began online, compared to only 19 per cent between 2005 and 2014. Self-proclaimed 'Worst Online Dater' is an internet figure who has conducted social experiments to try to demystify dating algorithms, and his conclusion on Tinder, the world's most popular dating app with 55 billion matches to date, is that it 'can actually work, but pretty much only if you are an attractive guy'. He worked out that the bottom 80 per cent of men in terms of attractiveness were competing for the bottom 22 per cent of women, and that the top 78 per cent of women were competing for the top 20 per cent of men. Women swipe right less than men do and because of the way Tinder's algorithm works, a man of average attractiveness can only expect to be liked by slightly less than 1 per cent of women.

This chapter will probe the lives of men who feel like they are not embodying the uncompromising male success story of the virility myth. For some, the resulting despair will prompt them to turn on women, rather than the toxic masculinity forcing them into this role in the first place. For others, it will simply end their life. And for those who do successfully date, many are finding that the relentless pressure to embody the virility myth triggers so much performance anxiety that it is stopping us from healthily discussing and curing sexual dysfunction.

There is reason to worry about this. A US study of 600 men found that men who perceived themselves to be less masculine according to traditional gender norms could be more prone to violent behaviour. It's not that all men who feel that way become violent, it's just that for those who get actively stressed out about it – something that's called 'masculine discrepancy stress' – that stress can lead them to substance abuse, binge drinking, reckless driving, weapon carrying and violence. It is tempting to deploy the word 'incel' freely here, especially when the security threat that involuntary celibate ideology poses seems to be increasing and when it feels like governments aren't taking it seriously enough, but

this chapter demands nuance and radical empathy in a polar-
ised social media climate that often deprives us of them.
Before we use the word incel, we need to understand what it
means, who it is exactly we are criticising and – vitally – who
it is that needs help.

So what happens when sexual accomplishment and
masculinity are considered one and the same? And what
happens when men who desperately want to be seen as virile
fail in their quest?

*

The one thing that kept Andrew going was the idea that,
when he turned eighteen, he'd go to college. He did everything in his power to make that happen; his grandparents
set aside some money and he studied every day, all to make
sure he'd get offered a place somewhere. His mum and
dad fought constantly, and when Andrew couldn't get his
homework done on time in this stressful environment, his
teachers didn't help him. 'You're not going to get into college if you're this lazy,' they would say to him in front of the
whole class.

This was the late 2000s; at the turn of the decade,
Andrew's parents still couldn't give him cable TV or high-
speed internet. At school, kids would talk about MySpace,
Charlie the Unicorn, *The OC*. Andrew couldn't join in. He
couldn't connect with them. One day his grandfather asked
him over their roast chicken and potatoes, 'Andrew, when
are you going to get a girlfriend?' Andrew had no idea.

College didn't prove to be any easier. 'I was so stressed out from my classes and schoolwork that I would spend the majority of my free time, whenever I wasn't with friends, in my apartment, surfing the web and hanging out on forums,' he tells me, 'which would hurt me in the long run. I studied engineering, so pretty much all of my classmates were male. I did have some friends who were successful romantically and dated and slept around a bunch. However, they never really gave me any advice. They'd just say, "Hey, just go talk to women," or, "Just figure that out on your own."'

He's found a sense of camaraderie in r/virgin, a subreddit (forum) for virgins who consider themselves 'older'. It is supposed to be a supportive community, but a lot of the language is despairing and most of the users posting are male; some are as young as sixteen. 'Knowing I'm unloveable hurts,' writes one. 'Is anyone else putting themselves in the friendzone on purpose because you know you'll never be good enough?' writes another.

'I don't hate women or want them dead, or any fucked-up shit,' Andrew tells me. 'But I definitely feel frustrated and resentful of my situation, and I think it can carry over. I hate having to lie. I hate having my worth completely tied to it; other people, including women, can dismiss all of my other accomplishments and traits because of my lack of experience.

'It's black magic to me, at this point. Nobody can give me a straight answer on what I need to do. It's not like I want to seduce women and have a bunch of one-night stands, I just want one I find attractive to like me back like that. I know it sounds terrible, but I don't know how a woman can decide that some random other guy is "fuckable" and not me. It just feels like people are intentionally hiding the key to feeling like a normal human being, like they want me to feel down.'

*

A lot has been written in recent years about incel culture, the internet landscape of men who feel like they cannot access the 'sexual marketplace' but long to. Being unable to perform the virility myth's ideal doesn't, however, stop them from believing in other traditional masculine norms. Research remains nascent, although the most comprehensive literature review that has been done so far (which is a preprint released in September 2021, not yet peer reviewed) found that incels share many psychological tendencies with adult virgins and adults who have their first sexual experiences late in life, and these groups have been studied far more comprehensively. The author of the review explains how existing literature on adult male virgins can reveal more about incel development: 'With life course theory, which stresses the importance of transitioning in sync with one's peers, being "off time" relative to others, whether too early or too late, has been shown to be associated with negative social and psychological consequences.' Andrew, like many, is terrified of being an incel – but he has already started employing the language of one, by framing women, and not the pressures of hegemonic masculinity, as the problem.

People like Andrew, who are quietly lulled into feelings of hopelessness and a dislike of women, aren't necessarily who come to mind when we picture an 'incel'; only covered in the media when they commit a violent crime, our image of inceldom is one of terror. The horrors of incel massacres, such as the Plymouth shooting in 2021, galvanise otherwise open-minded people on the internet to condemn the actions of men they brand loners and virgins, thus always associating incels with violent misogyny, when in reality their online world is more porous and diverse, also including people who are simply lonely. The weirdness of deploring one's own virginity in online manifestos is fetishised by the media, without pausing to think how reading such articles might make other non-violent, lonely male virgins feel. There is a real quandary here for journalists, who need to navigate two scenarios: alerting the world to a very real threat from men who build their identity around their inability to have sex, while reminding readers that not all young, inexperienced men espouse these ideas, and that there is nothing wrong with being a virgin or indeed feeling lonely. This is especially urgent given that modern trends suggest that men remain virgins for longer and are having less sex.

This nuance, acceptance and solutions-oriented outlook can rarely be found in online incel spaces. Self-loathing virgins who believe women are the problem penetrate online forums that aren't even about incel culture in the first place but are more broadly focused on masculine self-improvement. NoFap, originally a community for those trying to abstain from masturbation, sex and pornography, was found by researchers to promote the idea that women were 'toxic and undateable', 'thots' and 'roasties', and encouraged men to cure themselves of 'oneitis', a made-up condition in which men fawn over just one woman – a little like how men insult one another in mainstream online spaces for 'simping'. The researcher Scott Burnett observes that, despite railing against women, incels paradoxically posit heterosexual marriage as one of their goals: 'the figure of the "trad wife" who knows her proper social role . . . is the ultimate reward for the alpha masculinity facilitated by masturbation abstention'. Go to other, smaller spaces that focus on improving appearances, such as the subreddit (forum) r/looksmaxxing, where men mainly post selfies and ask how they could look better, and no one seems to suggest that there are many ways one can bolster self-esteem and develop well-rounded qualities that might help them find a partner. I am struck by how many men on there look totally normal but call themselves 'genetic trash' and consider facial surgery. One of them is rated 6/10 by a user, who tells them he has 'an unideal eye area' and 'flat cheekbones'. Someone else says 'dye your hair black and give your skin a yellower tone with betacarotene supplements'. By disappearing into the internet wormhole of these forums, young men aren't accessing genuinely useful advice about how to navigate power and gender dynamics in the modern world. Instead, they are confirming their suspicions that they are ugly and unwanted, based only on how they look.

The vast majority of male virgins do not become violent terrorists, but with so many of them finding nowhere else that's accepting to talk about their sexlessness, it is obvious that incel and incel-adjacent online spaces offer a sense of affirming community away from an outside world that calls them creeps. In the r/virgin subreddit, I find many men are also subscribed to Forever Alone forums, which do what they say on the tin – provide a place for people who are not simply currently feeling lonely but anticipate they will be lonely for the rest of their lives. The ratio of sound advice, compared to comments reeking of misanthropy, is distressingly low.

There is one forum I find, however, that is a little different: r/IncelExit. While it's still full of young men despairing over their sexual inactivity, they come to the forum for support rather than to wallow in self-pity. With over 7,000 members, it calls itself a place 'for people who got drawn into the incel community but want support and help with a way out'. In it, I find one user who seems to spend hours a day commenting under the various new calls for help – and I discover that he's actually a psychology PhD student called Chris.

'I'm not entirely sure why I ended up spending so much time in r/IncelExit specifically,' he tells me. 'But it did resonate with me in some way. I've never been anything close to the current stereotype of an incel, but I was a "late bloomer" and definitely empathise with feeling unattractive to the opposite sex, and the feelings of unworthiness that come with that.'

Chris spends hours a week on Reddit, but especially on this subreddit. He thinks that a lot of the incels there fall into the same camp. 'Not necessarily hateful, but just feeling awful about themselves and their failure to live up to what they see as being the "normal" standards that society sets for them.' I tell Chris about a paper from 2020 that I've come across in the *Journal of Positive Sexuality*, which describes incel ideology as 'extreme sex-negativity' and suggests in its conclusion that 'widespread education and promotion of positive sexuality principles would seem to help, over time, in mitigating multiple risk factors for such extreme violence fuelled by sex-negativity'. I ask him if he thinks sex education, or a dearth of it, might have anything to do with this. 'I do see a hell of a lot of misconceptions around – not just sex itself, but also sexual attraction,' Chris ponders. 'They pin all their problems on their lack of sex, which ironically stops them from moving forward in a way that would actually lead to them getting it. Some education on things like how frequently people are having sex, how important it is to their relationships [and] life overall . . . would probably be helpful. Different types of relationships as well: dominant male, dominant female, same-sex, asexual . . . anything that can help people move on from the idea that "I'm only a real man if women want to fuck me just by looking at me".'

But he thinks helping men out of the incel community would take a lot more than sex education. 'Lack of sex is only one part of what makes incels incels. There are always other problems that need to be addressed, like poor self-esteem, a lack of friends or capacity to socialise, an inability to make genuine intimate connections with other people, a poor self-image that trends towards body dysmorphia, a lack of social contact with women.' Taking all that into consideration, it's clear that better sex education can be part of helping people but is not the entire solution.

Although Chris spends a lot of time on the subreddit himself, he thinks the best thing that users can do is get off the computer and go into the real world, get hobbies and find a therapist. 'I am of the opinion that well-adjusted, healthy people don't spend large amounts of time posting hateful content online, so you're more likely to find those kinds of people out in the real world,' he says aptly. 'It was common on the old incel subs to see them posting compilations of tweets quoting women who had said stuff like "short men should die" and use that as evidence that women have some kind of irrational hatred for short people. You and I would recognise that as being the extreme views of particularly hateful or insecure people, and not at all representative of the world in general, because we've had enough interactions with women to know that that's not how normal people act. But incels have often already had a few bad interactions with women and start with the mindset of "women are bad" in the first place. Confirmation bias then takes over, they search for something hateful that they think women would say, and then, hey presto, there's the evidence that they were right all along, women are terrible people, and all the ones who don't act terrible online are just pretending.'

*

If you are a heterosexual woman reading this, you have probably *not* declared that all short men should die. But it is possible you have made or laughed at jokes about short men, small penises, men who can't get it up and men who don't last long. We don't call out virgin-shaming like we do slut-shaming – and with all the misogynistic content out there, it can be tempting to respond with a diatribe that hits the male ego where it hurts. But is that the answer? With the appalling state of male mental health, the rate of male sexual dysfunction and the unnerving backwaters of the internet encroaching on the real world, could we all be a little kinder?

Men could be helped if they were given more diverse, realistic depictions of male happiness that decentred virility. Sex researcher Sarah Hunter Murray interviewed thirty heterosexual men in relationships and found that lots of them had attached a high sex drive specifically to their male identity – leaving little room for anyone with a low sex drive, or anyone experiencing unreliable erections. Michael, aged thirty-three, said: 'I'm pretty much ready all the time . . . maybe we do have this biological system and maybe out in the wild we're like animals and stuff. Males will have multiple partners to provide for babies or whatever. So it could be a long, evolved system that we have, to be ready when it's time.' Thomas, who is fifty-five, said: 'I think it's how guys are built.'

But as she started to unpick some of these ideas with the interviewees, most of them also said they sometimes feigned desire to appear more masculine. 'Look at the TV shows and the music videos,' said Tim, a thirty-two-year-old. 'YouTube and stuff. Guys are supposed to be surrounded by women. Women aren't supposed to have their clothes on around them. Even that message speaks to [the idea that] . . . all guys want is naked women all around them all the time, right?' Some men felt they had to keep up appearances for their female partners who bought into the idea that men should be sexual initiators. 'So if I'm not doing that, I think she feels sexually inadequate. So sometimes I'll feign sexual desire even if I'm not into it just so she feels good about herself.' Joseph, aged thirty-seven, also felt some of the received wisdom around male sexual desire was suspect. 'The whole thing that men think about sex every seven and a half seconds is crap. I mean, we'd literally get nothing done. It's just insane. Like, we wouldn't be able to cook anything proper. We'd depend on the microwave.'

*

In the media, there is a campaign called the Clit Test, in which a film or song passes or fails based on whether it references clitoral stimulation or only penetrative sex. The same might be said of men too. Think about how many sex scenes you've watched; how often have you seen soft or semi-soft penises, in need of a moment or two of further stimulation? Apart from the kind of power blow jobs written into scripts like *The Sopranos*, the focus on penetrative sex on screen doesn't allow space for men without erections. This is nothing new. In the Ancient Roman city of Pompeii, walk into the house of the Vettii, a family that epitomised new money, and in the entrance you will, all these millennia later, be welcomed by a fresco of Priapus. Believed to ward off bad luck and usher in fertility, this Greco-Roman god has a penis so large and erect that he is weighing it on a pair of scales.

Erectile dysfunction (ED) affects up to one in five men across the UK, and prescriptions for Viagra and other ED drugs have tripled in Britain in a decade. A Co-op Pharmacy survey of 2,000 men suggested that 50 per cent of men in their thirties are struggling with it, and a study of under-forties in Brazil has found that the condition was more common in eighteen to twenty-five-year-olds than those aged twenty-six to forty. While causes can be anatomical, drug-related or a product of narrow blood vessels, the most common in young men is anxiety, which can develop at any time.

'We don't see soft penises anywhere!' declared Dr Silva Neves, a London-based sex therapist. 'The pressure of being sexually potent and a great lover is tied into their masculinity, and feeling like in order to be a man, you need to have an erection all the time. If we see men who are naked, it's usually men with erections. We don't see diverse types of penises. It's usually large and rock hard . . . the pressure for body perfection and sexual potency is so high. So many have erection problems.'

Dr Neves explains that men can get themselves into an anxiety loop similar to women who experience vaginismus. In the same way I used to expect and fear pain but pray that this time it wouldn't hurt, and then it inevitably would, men with erectile dysfunction couldn't get it hard last time, so they're dreading it's going to happen again, and it does. This vicious circle shows how inextricably connected the penetration and virility myths are. I ask Dr Neves if he thinks doctors are taking anxiety seriously enough when a patient comes in with ED.

'At the moment, a lot of GPs don't do all the tests required,' he explains. 'I've got a lot of clients who say they've been given Viagra and I ask them, "What tests did they do?" and they just say that they had no tests. The doctor just told them they were very young to be getting erectile dysfunction, and to just take Viagra. But an erection problem could be because of an undetected heart problem, early onset diabetes, low testosterone.' If those tests don't find any physical cause, the patient is often still given Viagra. 'But they'll come out with pills and without addressing the cause . . . for Viagra to work you need sexual arousal. If you have too much anxiety, that arousal might not happen.'

The same disinvestment of sexual and psychosexual health services that affects vaginismus sufferers obviously affects men too, but there are also other issues at hand. Men are far less likely to speak to a doctor about sexual problems than women are, so many of them will be skipping the doctor entirely. The Co-op survey found that only around a quarter of those interviewed with erectile dysfunction had gone to their GP about it and just 9 per cent had discussed it with another man in their family. Given that in the past year an estimated 42 per cent of British men would have had a sexual problem lasting three months or longer, that means there could be a huge number of men feeling too ashamed to seek medical help for an eminently curable condition – all because it makes them feel less manly.

You can now buy Viagra over the counter in the UK, meaning that men who suspect they have erectile dysfunction may attempt to self-medicate. Couple that with the fact that a 2015 study found that 12.5 per cent of men with sexual disorders also had depression, and nearly a quarter of them had anxiety. That means there are a lot of people with anxiety who are getting over-the-counter Viagra assuming they have a blood-flow problem, or whose doctors are misunderstanding the psychological element of their issues, and the pill isn't working because their difficulty isn't in fact *physical*.

Instead of receiving sympathy from partners, some men face derision, as happened with a patient of Dr Neves. 'He stood in the bedroom and froze – he hadn't told his female partner he was a virgin, and he knew that she had had sex before, and so thought he'd just get through it and pretend that he knew how to perform. That's how he treated it, a performance. But the erection never came, and when he looked up at her, she raised an eyebrow and he immediately started to apologise. And that's how his anxiety loop began.'

Dr Silva Neves has become one of the therapists to work with Mojo, a new online platform for 'reliable erections', where men can get remote support for erectile dysfunction. One of the co-founders, Angus Barge, has come across negative virginity-loss experiences time and time again on Mojo's forums and group webinars. 'Men losing their virginity is an anxious feeling . . . As soon as you know you've got to put on a show, it's fight or flight.'

Angus runs the platform with his cousin, Xander, whose own erectile dysfunction began when he tried to lose his virginity. During Freshers' Week, Xander thought that the girl he had managed to take back to his halls was much more experienced than he was and he got nervous. 'The fact that it didn't go well was enough to make him worry the second time that it wasn't going to go well,' says Angus. 'Fast forward ten years and he's in a car with me, telling me about it because we've shared for the first time with each other that we both had erectile dysfunction.'

Angus's experience was different, and more physiological; he crushed blood vessels in his perineum during a cycling event in Mallorca. 'Had I left it alone, it would have fixed itself in six to twelve weeks,' he explains. 'But I went home with someone and just couldn't get it up.'

After their mutual epiphany, Angus and Xander decided that support for young men with erectile dysfunction needed not only dramatic improvement, but liberated conversation. 'Seventy-five per cent of men will never seek professional help if they have a sexual dysfunction, though the vast majority want it,' said Angus. 'The mental health landscape has changed over the last fifteen to twenty years. Men's mental health is harder to crack. Xander and I see sexual health as intrinsically linked to mental health. It's the next frontier.' Angus pauses. 'I'm trying to think back to when I was at uni. I had friends who'd say that they couldn't get it up but it was only ever in the context of drinking. We did market research about their experience of it and loads of guys in the street would say, "Yeah, I've had that – only when I'm drunk though."'

Angus says that most of their user base, which is already international, having launched only a few months ago, come to Mojo because they're starting some form of new relationship. 'They like the person, they want to get it right. You'd think that guys come to us because they need to fix this, want to have sex, but actually a lot of people do it because they think, *she'll leave me*. It's more to satisfy your partner than it is yourself. Which is sad, because it should be fun, it should be a special experience for you . . . It's not just so you can maintain a relationship.' Interestingly, that same Co-op survey found that 27 per cent of respondents claimed that they would rather break up with their partner than talk to their GP about being unable to get an erection. Men are so reluctant to open up about sexual dysfunction that the only person they seem to trust with this information is themselves.

Angus tells me that men like the anonymity an online forum like Mojo affords. 'I turned to forums when I was struggling,' he says. 'One of the most widely used resources that isn't professional help is Reddit forums. Although they're great at helping you feel like you aren't isolated, they aren't professional. It's personal advice and guidance when you don't know someone's background.' He had seen advice that included 'thrashing yourself with nettles because that increases blood flow'.

As previously mentioned, a vast number of men online associate their erectile problems with porn consumption and masturbation, and have found what seems to be a potential solution in the #NoFap movement, which promotes sexual abstention because its believers hope that decreasing their reliance on masturbating will make them healthier men and/or better in bed, as the virility myth demands of them. No Nut November, a month-long challenge that originated in the subreddit, now even enters mainstream media coverage every year. Whether your goal is casual participation in a month-long challenge as a test of self-control, or whether excessive masturbation or pornography has become a problem in your life and you want to quit for a longer period of time, you will find a supportive community and plenty of resources here.

There's reason to be concerned about men going to these forums first, rather than a doctor. Firstly, not masturbating at all is not what doctors recommend in treating erectile dysfunction; masturbating isn't going to hurt you and actually comes with health benefits such as stress reduction, better sleep and relieving muscle tension, on which abstainers will miss out. Abstainers might also be pathologising behaviours that aren't actually addictions; porn addiction still doesn't actually exist in the International Classification of Diseases, and research has also found that you're more likely to think you're an addict if you morally disapprove of porn. Josh Grubbs, a leading behavioural researcher in this field, told me: 'It's normally really hard to get addicts to admit to being addicts. So why are there all these people on the internet declaring that they're porn addicts?'

This suggests that some of them experience feelings of shame around their porn use, which influences their views on other problems they might be having, something that Dr Neves thinks needs to be interrogated in therapy. He explains to me how he has often taught men to masturbate in a different way that is essentially less vigorous, and more like penetrative sex with a partner. Lastly, he recommends communication, even if you feel like it's not 'manly' to instigate it. I say to him: 'I can understand how it might be easier to talk to a long-term partner about erectile dysfunction, but a casual partner? It must be even more terrifying.'

'If you say, "I've got an erection problem," it takes the fun away,' he concedes. 'But if instead you say, "Hey, I'd really like us to just be together with our bodies. These are the parts of my body I like to use; which parts would you like me to touch?" – first of all, you might relax the partner, but you also give the clear message that the important bit is what we are going to make and do together.' He smiles broadly. 'And that is exciting! The message is: don't focus on my penis. Have sex with me, not my penis.'

If men really are feeling like porn is damaging their real-life relationships, it's a vicious cycle; in a world in which porn-viewing is not only often defined as a masculine activity but as one which young men are encouraged to partake in because they are young men, the virility myth's compulsion to consume it and then perform pornographic sex on women sets many up with unrealistic expectations for real-world sex. It's a virility ouroboros, consuming itself and getting men nowhere. It is perpetuating the myth that they have control, when what they have is sexual autonomy and agency – just like women should. Hardly anyone I know in my age group, male *or* female, feels in control of their lives; a pandemic and inflation remind me every day of how little I control, and that's before we get onto systemic injustices towards different communities.

In 2020, the Office of National Statistics reported an increasing proportion of young people aged sixteen to twenty-four in the UK who were finding it difficult or very difficult to get by financially, particularly among young men. While men are less likely to experience anxiety and depression than women, suicide is a far higher killer of men, and they are less likely to talk about such feelings. It means that, for them, anxiety, depression and the almost inevitable impact such mental health issues have on sex lives go unrecognised and untreated. Our fascination with incels and the oddities of #NoFap are glaring beacons calling us to consider these problems more seriously; we can do better than to instantly vilify or name-call.

Over the last month, there have been over forty posts in r/suicidewatch where users reference their virginity. 'Is there any point continuing to live if you turn twenty and are still a virgin?' someone asks. Another twenty-year-old virgin reaches out in a reply. 'I did think about killing myself over this for some time,' they admit. 'But sex is not everything. Think about it. How do you think it would help you to have sex?' The original poster consents to a DM, and, hopefully, they had a chat.

It's eleven days later now, and he hasn't posted since.

6

The Sexlessness Myth

It normally takes Malik about five hours of sitting in a chair before he's ready to do his job. Sometimes he gets new teeth for it – other times it's new hair, new skin. Sometimes they take away his nose.

'I played a gorilla for the Eden Project last year,' he says. 'It was super easy. Easy and clear, no pretence there.' He calls himself a 'creature actor', specialising in the performance of non-humans, fictional or real. He tells me that he really enjoyed the award-winning *The Shape of Water*, a love story between a woman and an 'amphibian man', and often finds it harder to play humans. 'I can relate to that idea, of performing a creature that might fall in love. It's easier to visualise as a performer, not as a person. The more make-up I wear, the further I can remove myself. That [playing a creature], for me, would be easier to perform.'

But there are other performances that Malik hasn't enjoyed. 'I was supposed to kiss the female lead. I'm really not into kissing, it grosses me out. I don't think I've ever felt so awkward in my entire life – I had no preparation.'

Since his early twenties, Malik has been consuming more and more information around asexuality, a little-understood sexual identity in which people find they have no compulsion to have sex or sexual relationships. Asexuality covers a broad range of experiences. It is in fact so broad that many in the community call themselves 'aces': possibly asexual, or possibly another identity pertaining to asexuality within its spectrum. Some might want romantic relationships without the sex; others aren't remotely interested in any kind of partnership whatsoever. Statistically speaking, you as a random member of the general population are probably allosexual – but you've never realised it before, because you've never needed to describe yourself or define that identity to anyone. To be allosexual means that you experience sexual desire and attraction.

Asexuality, its stigma and our lack of general awareness offer a very clear example of how much we assume that everyone on the planet wants to have sex. Not only do a lot of us accept this as fact, but when someone says that they don't want to have or seek sex, many of us struggle to understand why. For some people, it's not *normal* to not want sex. That is a very short-sighted and often offensive view. Within the vast spectrum of our diverse sexual identities, sexualities and fluctuating libidos, it is perfectly normal to not want to have sex. For some, it's for a delineated period of time; for others, it could be a life choice, or it could simply be the way that we are, as is the case for asexuals.

The sexlessness myth – that there is something odd about not having or wanting sex, and that your life must be deficient as a result – is very much alive in the twenty-first century, despite the fact that we are supposed to be more inclusive and accepting of varied sexual experiences, LGBTQIA and otherwise. In many cases, the medical community is still pathologising such experiences, seeing low or absent sexual desire as something to cure rather than as a natural part of ourselves. In this chapter, I'm not discussing the sexlessness of sexual immaturity and inexperience; I'm considering the wilful decisions to be sexless that aren't impacted by disapproval around premarital sex. I am thinking of the adults who, experienced or not, designate periods of their life or even their whole lifetimes to eschew relational, partnered sex. Here, we witness interesting overlaps with other sex myths, such as the need to be seen as sexually active or be partnered, as we saw in the virginity myth and the virility myth. The stigmatised in those chapters felt like their sexlessness was the root cause of their alienation, but this chapter suggests something quite different. It is a chapter of people empowered by their sexlessness, in spite of everything a sex-obsessed society tells them.

By its very construct, 'sexlessness' sounds negative, implying someone is lacking something. That is the fault of the English language, I'm afraid, which doesn't offer us much flexibility. To simply call someone who doesn't have sex celibate is misguided; what if they're asexual, in which case this isn't a choice, but a sexual orientation? What if they aren't religious, in which case they might take issue with the connotations of celibacy? Even the word 'abstaining' feels like co-opting religious language and suggests that sex is addictive like alcohol, when it's not. We might then simply be left with words such as single, bachelor and, God forbid, spinster. Again, unpartneredness becomes the focus, in a world where marriage and relationships are the normative social goals. But if we expand our understanding of the many identities in which intercourse is not an assumed part of our sexuality, we may, if we dare, allow ourselves to see a wider picture of sex positivity and sexual autonomy: one where we are in control of defining our sex(less) lives, rather than letting *them* define *us*.

It's not an easy feat, mind you; sex and romance are everywhere. Often, sex's place in our life isn't just about sexual activity, but what it symbolises. A sense of union, or wholeness; the opposite of loneliness. Malik now knows that he sits somewhere between gay and asexual, and has long felt alienated by popular culture. 'Most, if not all, films, in general say that you're not complete until you find someone else. The happy ending is that the Disney prince gets the princess and is now complete. The narrative that I do find quite offensive sometimes is when people say that the LGBTQIA community is pushing an agenda. But all these people have been indoctrinating all of us! That you're not complete unless you have a relationship!' He pauses and laughs. 'Maybe it played into my initial ideas about who I needed to be, that I needed to have someone else. Thinking beyond asexuality, beyond aromanticism, there is something great when you just totally click with someone. But it doesn't mean that everyone needs that to be happy.'

A number of articles claim that asexuality is the first 'internet orientation'. The suggestion that it has only existed in the age of the internet is inaccurate, but it does rightly point to the flourishing of ace communities online – communities that had no previous offline counterpart. If you compare gay or lesbian subcultures, you can track extensive pre-internet histories and communities; with asexuality, it's a bit trickier. It has taken time for asexuality to be considered a sexual orientation across LGBTQIA, medical, legal and academic communities. New York holds the only piece of legislation in the world – the Sexual Orientation Non-Discrimination Act – that mentions asexuality.

A lack of these supposedly 'inherent' feelings has meant that asexuality suffers from an ongoing history of being pathologised. 'I'm not attracted to anyone' has usually elicited such responses as 'there must be something wrong with you or your libido' from healthcare professionals, rather than 'that's interesting, perhaps you're asexual?' It was only in February 2021 that someone in Wikipedia's edit history plucked 'asexuality' out of libido's 'disorders' section. In the past, some people who were in reality asexual may have instead been diagnosed with Hypoactive Sexual Desire

Disorder. Charli Clement, an asexual activist who is also disabled and autistic, said that she's often been medically misunderstood. 'For me, there's an intersectionality of my disability and asexuality activism because both identities are commonly infantilised and it is often assumed I am asexual due to my autism, which isn't accurate.'

In 2014, the Tumblr account vaginismusandsexuality, whose founder has suffered from vaginismus and identifies as asexual, said: 'My counsellor told me to have sex until I like it and to have various medical tests to see what was wrong with me; my doctor prescribed me three different medications, two of which have been clinically proven to have no significant effect on ciswomen (Viagra and Cialis, the third was a testosterone supplement). I should not have to discuss the emotional turmoil it has put me through and what it has done to me.'

Until as recently as 2013, a lack of sexual desire was defined as a disorder in the *Diagnostic and Statistical Manual of Mental Disorders* in the US. But members of the Asexuality Visibility Education Network, which formed in the early 2000s, went to the American Psychiatric Association and presented a seventy-eight-page report they had written, consolidating information and a literature review on asexuality. In 2013, Hypoactive Sexual Desire Disorder disappeared. It was replaced by Female Sexual Interest/Arousal Disorder and Male Hypoactive Sexual Desire Disorder. The entries for both these newly named disorders say: '[I]f a lifelong lack of sexual desire is better explained by one's self-identification as "asexual", then a diagnosis of FSAID or MHSDD would not be made.'

The use of quotation marks for 'asexual' here has been criticised by some, but a rather more glaring problem is that in order to self-identify as asexual, you need to actually know what asexuality is, and lots of people have still never heard of the term. The international medical community remains divided on this front; the International Classification of Diseases continues to omit any mention of asexuality in its information on sexual desire dysfunctions. When I type 'no libido' into the NHS website, the only options offered are a 'loss of libido' or 'menopause'. For those questioning whether they experience desire or not and whether they should be worried about it or understand it, there isn't a single link on either page that directs individuals towards information on asexuality. Instead, they might confirm the societal bias that something is wrong with them.

The low levels of awareness around asexuality mean that many people who are asexual do not realise it until several years into their sexual maturity, and those who aren't asexual hopelessly misunderstand it. In 2019, a poll by Sky Data tested UK adults on their confidence in defining asexuality; of over 1,000 people questioned, 53 per cent said that they were confident in explaining the term, but when they were actually put to the test, 75 per cent of them were either wrong or didn't know that some asexual people can have a sex drive. So a lot of us *think* we know what asexuality is, without having really done the homework to understand it.

A 2012 study found a strong bias against asexual people in the general population – so much so that asexual people were viewed more negatively than those who identify as homosexual or bisexual, two groups that have long been marginalised. Asexuals were also seen as the least 'human'. In another study from 2007, asexual people reported that they had lower health risks and more free time compared to non-asexuals. Yet non-asexuals were likely to pathologise this, and believe that asexuals were missing out on the positive aspects of sex. If you make asexuals feel negative about their sexlessness, rather than minding your own business, what effect does that have? In the UK's largest ever survey on the LGBTQIA community with over 108,000 participants, asexual and pansexual people had the lowest life satisfaction scores compared to any other sexual orientation. They were also the least comfortable with being LGBTQIA and being open about their sexuality in public.

*

When Otto first came out as gay and downloaded Grindr, the world that was there waiting for them wasn't necessarily something that they were on board with. 'The gay world is hyper-sexualised,' they tell me now, years later. 'Obviously you can find romance on there, but it's primarily for sex. And everything on there was hyper-sexualised, but also hyper-aestheticised.'

This is coming from Otto, who is probably the most aesthetically minded person I know and can often be found in a grand assortment of wigs, masks and bling on nights out. 'I've found the queer space more diverse and accepting, but the gay world pushed me from that scene. I was like, why am I not feeling all these desires to sleep with all these men? I thought that maybe I'm broken, maybe I'm not gay or queer enough.'

Otto wasn't broken or lacking in anything. What they were was asexual – they just hadn't realised it at that point. They would go on to identify as non-binary too, and now, years later, they understand that it's their body that knows best for them. 'It doesn't mean I don't have sexual thoughts, but the thought of having sex with someone is generally quite abhorrent to me,' Otto explains, telling me that this doesn't mean they don't feel sexual desire, or a lack of interest in having a partner. They are worried, though, that a future partner might have sexual demands that jar with theirs. 'If you think about desire and someone's energy,' Otto says, 'if [one partner's] is way stronger, there is automatically going to be a deficit. The difficulty is how you address it. Or do I need to find someone with a similar degree of it?'

Otto pauses, reflecting on their time on Grindr. 'It's all very well finding a long-term partner on Tinder or Hinge for hookups, but what is there for asexuality? I haven't really searched it. I want the option, but not the expectation, to have sex.'

When the Trevor Project surveyed over 40,000 LGB-TQIA youth, they found that 10 per cent identified as asexual or somewhere on the ace spectrum, and that they reported higher rates of depression and anxiety compared to the overall LGBTQIA sample. The Trevor Project writes that 'while not everyone who is asexual wishes to be part of the LGBTQIA community, LGBTQIA youth who are asexual are an often-overlooked group. These results show that most asexual youth who identify with the LGBTQIA community endorse a range of sexual and romantic orientations.' The project concludes from its findings that 'efforts must be made to include asexual youth in LGBTQIA youth outreach and in suicide prevention and intervention efforts'.

Yet several asexuals I have spoken to have encountered hostility from LGBTQIA individuals, especially if they otherwise identify as cisgender and heteroromantic. I interviewed one man in his thirties, Giovanni, who identifies as gay and demisexual, and like my friend Otto found that lots of gay men he had met had refused to accept that asexuality might qualify as a queer identity. Giovanni tweeted that he wished he could put both gay and demisexual down on the census, but that it only offered room to write down a singular sexual identity. 'I got pushback on it, all from gay men, and I was really shocked at the animosity. People were completely dismissing it as an identity or were complaining that every preference needs its own identity now.'

His interview was included in a piece I wrote about asexuality for BBC Three, which provoked a lot of pushback on Twitter, this time from seemingly straight individuals. The headline, 'I hoped I could repress my asexuality', was a quote from one of the contributors about their past, and not one I had chosen. One woman who saw it tweeted: 'No one cares if you're asexual or not. Why don't you get together with all the other flag waving narcissists and form your own victim support group?' A man posted: 'You can't repress something that isn't there.'

From their public profiles, I could gather that they were all of a certain age and unlikely to ever change their minds, unless they suddenly found themselves in a sex education programme for adults, or miraculously woke up one morning and realised how unenlightened they were. But it's not too late for you, or me, to do the homework that we need to do. Go to asexuality resources such as the Asexuality Visibility and Education Network and you will find a whole host of vocabulary to define the spectrum of ace sexual and romantic experiences:

Abroromantic – someone who fluctuates between experiencing romantic attraction and not experiencing it, or experiences it to different strengths

Lithosexual – someone who experiences sexual attraction to people, but has no desire to have these feelings reciprocated

Apothisexual – a person who is both asexual and sex-repulsed

Cupioromantic – someone who does not experience romantic attraction but has a desire to be in a romantic relationship

Demisexual – someone who can only experience sexual attraction after establishing a close emotional and/or romantic connection with other people

Frayromantic – someone who experiences romantic attraction, but this attraction fades after getting to know the object of attraction

Grey-sexual – a catch-all term for those who sit somewhere in the limbo between asexuality and allosexuality

The many colours of asexuality and aromanticism invite a level of introspection that I don't think I have ever had to apply to myself as a cisgender, heterosexual woman. By furrowing neatly into what is largely expected of me in heteronormative society, I have never had to question why I fell for this man or why I got bored with that man. But when you find that you live in a cardboard cut-out world of love, sex and passion that you don't feel a part of, it's not surprising that so many people feel alone.

Charli Clement told me that, at first, her parents didn't understand what asexuality was, but now they have sought out more information about it. 'Back in 2014, I tested the waters and mentioned asexuality in a discussion with them, and my parents thought it had to be something to do with a hormone imbalance or something similar,' she explains. 'I ended up coming out to my mum on a random car journey, and I came out publicly on Instagram on Coming Out Day the same year. My family are so supportive and have never made me feel weird or broken or put pressure on me to have relationships. People tell me I was too young to know, but I think that implies that we have to have had sex to decide we're asexual.'

*

Just a few streets back from the seafront stands the Cathedral of the Good Shepherd of San Sebastián. It's the biggest one in the province, which is, admittedly, the smallest province in Spain, but it still looms with the grandeur and quiet superiority that Neo-Gothic architecture commands. If you walk around the back of the churchyard and turn left, you'll see the diocese bookshop where you will find the smiling Maria Pagalday, who knows the books here like the back of her hand. And on that very hand is a wedding ring – but you'd be hard pressed to find her husband. That's because, technically speaking, he's everywhere. His name is Jesus Christ – and Maria is one of his 5,000 earthly brides.

His name is inscribed inside the gold band, just like a husband's or wife's would be: *Jesucristo*, in cursive handwriting, like she wrote it there herself. She was twenty-nine when she decided to become a consecrated virgin, a vocation for Catholic women in which you pledge your perpetual virginity, and requisite lifelong celibacy, to Jesus Christ. 'In Spain there are about two hundred of us,' she tells me. 'When I consecrated myself some wrote to me, some of them even came to the consecration. There aren't any others here, but in other areas there's a bit of a community. We all meet once a year and we have a very active WhatsApp group.'

Much of Maria's life looks exactly the same as it did before she made this decision; she lives in the same place and spends plenty of time with her friends and family. 'Lots of people think that it's this huge decision, a great loss and that it's better to live without promising yourself to a false sense of freedom. I've discovered that the promise is done for love, that it's become a guardian of this love and has raised it. Since I promised myself in body and soul to God, I feel much more free in my relationship with God and everybody else.' Then she adds: 'Consecrated virginity is also a message to the world that reminds us that we are passing through this life and that the goal is Heaven. It's eternal life. It's God. We live this life to live eternally with God.' Lifelong virginity is a small price to pay for an eternity in paradise.

Although the church had a number of consecrated virgins as early as the third century CE, the phenomenon of consecrated virginity is fairly modern. A revival led by a small number of women resulted in consecrated virginity getting papal approval in 1970. In 2020, Pope Francis celebrated fifty years since the revised rite was promulgated. 'Your virginal consecration helps the Church to love the poor, to discern forms of material and spiritual poverty, to help those who are weak and vulnerable.' He said that they were 'women who believe in the revolutionary nature of love and tenderness'. As of 2018, there are approximately 5,000 virgins living in the world who are 'mystically betrothed to Christ'.

That you are defined by both your capacity for love *and* by your virginity contrasts sharply with secular ideas in which love is intimately bound with sexual desire and practice. But religious vocations like Maria's help us to understand that a life of no sex is by no means a life unfulfilled, nor one without fervour or romance.

Go online today and you will find many people of different traditions talking about their decision to become celibate. Of course, many of them are religious; in the English-speaking world, many appear to be Christians from the US, the UK and the African continent. A twenty-seven-year-old from Cameroon told me, 'I was in a relationship that many, including me, thought was going to end in marriage, but sadly things took a bad turn. I didn't decide to be celibate – well, not at first. I just didn't think I needed anything sensual for the first few weeks. Then weeks became months. Then it was easier being alone.'

He saw it as a period of romantic recovery: time to process and heal before moving on. For Aitana, who lives in East London and has been celibate since she turned seventeen, the recovery that celibacy offered her has meant a lot more than just a romantic reset. 'When I was younger, I was sexually molested by a family member and the idea that I can gain control over my body again and just focus on discovering every aspect of who I am and what makes me outside of sex really gave me a sense of peace that I desperately needed,' she explains. Around her waist, she wears beads, a replica of Vilanda necklaces from the Mwila tribe in Angola where her family originates. 'The women use beads as symbols of different stages of womanhood. The idea is that you wear them until you are married or you grow out of them. You wear the beads below the waist near your knicker line, so they're out of sight and your husband should be the man to see them. Over the years I've stacked them to commemorate each year of celibacy, but now I only wear one for comfort!'

Before she committed to being celibate, Aitana says that she was terrified of men. As she saw friends of hers begin to engage in casual sex, she got scared, for them and for herself. 'It made me very frigid,' she says. 'Sex genuinely terrified me. But as I started to read more into the Bible and what it has to say about sex being something fruitful, all of a sudden I was seeing sex linked with positive ideas. It helped me differentiate between the abuse I was victim of and the sex my friends were having. They were in control. They decided to have sex with people and were just enjoying their lives.

'I started to see myself differently; less like a victim, more like someone who is beautiful and deserving of love. When the time comes, I'll be ready and won't be living in the shadows of my trauma.'

Self-love and self-repair are topics commonly spoken of by celibates, and I find several heterosexual women online who connect their celibacy directly with the highs and lows of sexual liberation: an uneasy convergence where, despite being able to enjoy sexual freedom like men, women are still drawing the short straw of inequitable, unpleasurable casual sex, or experiencing difficulty finding long-term partners. A young woman who describes herself as spiritual and, having been celibate for seventeen months, dedicates an entire Instagram highlight to the subject, where she collects and shares tweets and posts that she identifies with. One tweet reads: 'Honestly idk how we went from destigmatising women being sexual beings, to equating sexual empowerment w/pleasing men & being appealing to men.' In response, she writes: 'Ask yourself why you're engaging in certain sexual activities, if it serves you, how it leaves you emotionally afterwards, if you're training to "gain" something. If you're more focused on performing for the man than you are on your own enjoyment, etc . . . Women have fallen into repurposed oppression in which men now encourage us to be sexual to our detriment.'

In some cases, the modern phenomenon of hookup culture *is* traumatic for women, especially if they feel like the sex that they're having isn't equitable in pleasure or respect. The coronavirus pandemic prompted interesting writing on celibacy, as if lockdown gave people the period of sexlessness that they never realised they needed and may not have sought for themselves had the pandemic not occurred. In an essay, writer Annie Lord explored how the absence of physical touch and the cooling of relentless dating had made her think more deeply about the nature of her desire and sense of self. Being unpartnered once made her feel less than whole, but during lockdown 'I have had to fill myself back up all on my own. Or as best as I can given the circumstances. Sweating into a bath. A book I can't put down. Running until my shins swell and endorphins make me forget everything that is bad.' She concludes that she misses the excitement of romance and physical touch, but that 'the difference is that now I don't need men to touch me to make me feel complete. I want them to touch me so they can see how complete I already am.'

Courtney, who lives in the West Midlands, relates to this too, having realised that lockdown forced her to address why she was putting herself in dangerous situations. 'I realised that I'd been using sex as self-harm,' she says, 'hooking up with randoms from Tinder every weekend and having shit sex that never satisfied me and would make me feel low and worthless afterwards.' She ties this explicitly to a lack of information about sex and body positivity at school, and says that the self-repair she's worked towards has come entirely from social media. 'I've since had opportunities to have sex, but I've chosen not to,' she smiles.

I ask her if she's noticed a trend that I've seen lately on TikTok, whereby users film videos of themselves in various outfits and describe themselves as 'written by a woman', and then 'written by a man'; the first may be more masculine, or have neon make-up, or anything that confounds traditional notions of female attractiveness, whereas the second will seem performed for the male gaze, perhaps with more make-up or tighter clothes. It's an understanding of gender performance I only really learned about at university when I studied Judith Butler, but with TikTok it looks like younger people are being taught about gender performance, and gender normativity, earlier. 'Yes!' exclaims Courtney. 'We're starting to see how ingrained the male gaze is in everything we consume!' Even though she isn't Muslim, she's also been following hijabi influencers who show her less revealing fitness wear, which she struggles to find on other accounts. 'I want to be respected for me; it isn't just for the pleasure of somebody else,' she says. It feels like a reckoning is underway: a body-positivity moment that isn't happening in a vacuum, but instead as a response to the everyday sexualisation of clothes and appearances. For people like Courtney, it is about more than choosing not to have sex – it is about rejecting sexual objectification.

It's also interesting how sexlessness in relationships, so often viewed as a sign of a relationship in decline, may not mean that, either. The Netflix series *Too Hot to Handle*, in which hot singles lose money from the prize fund if they have sexual contact with anyone in the villa, has become an antidote to programmes like *Love Island* that force people to couple sexually. Some of the more spiritual, 'find-yourself' segments in *Too Hot to Handle* are a bit saccharine, but its claim that couples will find a 'deeper connection' if they avoid constant sexual interactions is compelling. Several partners contact me to tell me that, in cohabiting with someone over an entire pandemic, they went through extended periods of sexlessness that, now the pandemic is largely over, have indelibly changed their sex lives. For one couple, who had stopped having intercourse and started having more oral and partnered masturbation instead, it's made them realise they don't need constant intercourse. Another couple tell me that they feel pent-up desire has helped them view sex as more fun and relaxed, rather than intensely important or serious. Many are realising that, as great as sex is, it's not the be-all and end-all of a relationship, or indeed a good time. This was backed up by the Natsal-COVID study that interrogated the effect of the pandemic on people's sex lives; while aspects of sex-life quality were more commonly reported to deteriorate, aspects of relationship quality were more commonly reported to improve. At a time when unfathomable external stressors forced us to change the way we live, some couples found themselves bolstered – not by sexual activity, but by their mutual support, love and connection beyond it.

I have thought about this a lot while writing this book and reflected on the many times that I have considered periods of celibacy, but ultimately ignored them – usually because I fancied someone new, and was always thrilled by that excitement. But now, I do wonder how different parts of my life might have looked if I had abstained from sex that was never going to be good in the first place. In some cases, it was never actually sex that I was after; it was companionship, and sometimes even power. With hindsight,

I look back at past versions of myself and see someone who was really quite lonely and powerless. Had someone spoken to me about celibacy, in a secular, sex-positive way, I might have found myself drawn to it.

It is also worth signposting that some people pursue celibacy because they are homosexual and their faith forbids same-sex relations while not totally forbidding a homosexual identity – i.e. you can be gay but not *act* gay. Many, particularly the non-religious, struggle to stomach this seeming internalising of homophobia and faith groups' cruel, anachronistic punishment of perfectly natural desires. But for those desperate to cling to these systems, and the support they think they find there, celibacy offers a way to maintain a queer identity and also establishes a link to their religion. This certainly does little to 'modernise' the concept of celibacy, or make it more palatable to those of us who are fighting for sex inclusivity.

I remain confident that there is a pathway for a non-religious celibacy that is sex positive: one where you can desire breaks from sex without needing to vilify it. Sadly, every person I spoke to who is celibate told me that they had been teased for their decision and labelled prudes and 'frigid'. Assuming that someone might be overtly concerned with decorum, propriety and *your* sexual behaviour simply because they have made the sexual choice of sexlessness isn't only wrong – it's insulting.

If we want to make more room for sex-positive celibacy for those who choose to pursue it for however long they like, a lot more of us are going to have to learn to respond with a bit more kindness – and a lot more open-mindedness.

*

'All I remember is somewhere during 6–7th grade, I would get repetitive intrusive thoughts about sex,' one teenager from Michigan tells me, in an Instagram group chat I have been invited into, arranged by the meme page @aromantic._.pride. 'I hated it, the idea of it made me want to hole up somewhere forever. When my mum joked about how I was eventually going to lose my virginity, I felt . . . not great lol. There was definitely a: "that's fucking weird, why would I do something like that?"' A seventeen-year-old non-binary person adds: 'For me, it was Year 10. I was having a conversation with a friend and they were talking about how they're attracted to their crushes and I realised I never really felt the same way before – that I've never felt that desire towards someone. I wasn't completely sure I was asexual as there isn't much representation or information in the media. But when I started looking at and following ace meme pages and figured out I could relate with them, I started to identify as asexual.'

Ivo, who is also seventeen, still isn't sure if he is asexual – but he does believe he is aromantic. 'A friend suggested I could be aro after I had spoken to him for a while about the fact I never had any crushes. It took me a few months after that to fully accept it.' He explains that he is not simply aromantic, but specifically cupioromantic – 'when you desire for a romantic relationship but don't experience romantic attraction'. I ask Ivo if he feels like it's challenging to find a partner. 'I would love a partner to be in a romantic relationship and I would love a partner to be romantic towards me, but if I'm not romantically attracted to them then that doesn't really work. It's not fair on them if I'm not reciprocating those feelings and I'm not sure how they would want to enter such a relationship in the first place.' But then later he adds: '[I]f I only view people as friends then why would I ever try to get into some kind of relationship if I don't have those intense feelings to urge me to pursue said relationship?'

Another user points out that 'there is another type of relationship we have too. It was created by the aromantic community! They're called queerplatonic partnerships (QPP) and they're sort of the grey area between friendships and romantic relationships. Typically they're committed relationships with two or more people, with the same commitment and affection of a romantic relationship but without the romance aspect. They're not the same as best friends as this is typically the person you will live with, marry, maybe even have kids with. However much the people in the relationship want to commit.' They themselves have been in a QPP for three years – 'It just so happened that my girlfriend was my childhood best friend and she is also aroace, so I understand how rare my circumstance was!'

This Instagram meme page is a small, aromantic utopia where these young people from all different walks of life can chat and laugh about their mutual identity. In its bio, it jokingly declares: 'CEO of No Romo'. Lots of the posts are memes, but others are educational: things young aromantics need to hear, myths about asexuality you need to know. One post, 'A safe post to vent', has 436 comments. Someone's cousin keeps telling them that they're just scared of sex; another is thirteen years old and her parents have told her that her demisexuality is just a result of 'online influence'. In a world of misunderstanding, the users in the comments have found the one thing that they have been denied not only in the wider world, but in the safety of their family homes: empathy.

In 2018, *The Atlantic* published an article titled 'Why are young people having so little sex?' The subheading said: 'Despite the easing of taboos and the rise of hookup apps, Americans are in the midst of a sex recession.' That is a peculiar way of framing sexlessness, which exists perhaps not in spite of sexual liberation, but *because* of it. The easing of taboos leads to a kinder world where we shouldn't feel pressurised to have sex at all. The trends that point to young people having less sex often attribute these to changes in society, namely moving out of your parents' home later, rising unemployment and spending more time in education. Not only are some of us prioritising work and school, but some of us are sensibly delaying sexual activity until we feel ready; many of us who feel like the onset of sexual activity came too early, or have suffered traumatic experiences since, consciously need sexlessness in order to recover. And lastly, for some of us, sexlessness is our life, but there is nothing about it that is 'less' at all. We're increasingly finding others who get it, and can now find company without the pressure of sex at all.

For many, the purpose of a sexual orientation is that you are sexually *directed* towards people of a certain group or identity, be it your own sex or gender, another sex or gender, or multiple sexes and genders; the idea that you might not point towards anyone or anything at all jars with that construct. We describe it as an orientation, as if love and sex were some kind of force that points to the object of our affection, which we simply charge towards. Yet I have rarely been the agent of my own amorous chaos – feelings have either emerged, or they have not. They have been and they have not been. An Arabic word for attraction, *al-hawa*, gives a sense of rising and falling like the breeze, which challenges our word attraction, from the Latin *attratere*, 'to pull'. Perhaps if we saw orientation as more ontological rather than active or something we have any sense of control over, we'd be better at understanding asexuality's position in it – as well as the natural ebb and flow of allosexual desire that allows us the time to breathe, and think, without the pressure of sexual activity.

7

The Consent Myth

I spent many afternoons at Durham University parked in a corner of the Swan and Three Cygnets, which overlooks the river. It was a pub that my boyfriend at the time and his friends were usually found at, where both locals and students jostled for torn leather seating. Anyone in my boyfriend's friendship group only needed to message the group chat with a rallying cry and they would all fly to the warm solace of the Swan, irrespective of whether they were in a lecture or not. The last to arrive had to buy the round as punishment for their tardiness and, remarkably, they all eventually graduated with good degrees.

One afternoon was a little different – their tones were hushed, half in awe, half in horror. Everyone was talking about something that had happened the night before. Two boys from their college had done 'the Houdini' – or at least tried to. I didn't know what the Houdini was. 'You have sex with a girl,' my boyfriend explained, 'and then with the lights turned off, you and a friend try to switch positions without the girl noticing.'

My boyfriend was not endorsing the practice, but somehow, in the whole group, there was a sense of conspiratorial joke-sharing as they saw off their pints. It was *funny*, and had been rendered even funnier by the fact that the second friend had farted in the wardrobe he was hiding in, revealing his presence and destroying the ruse – or at least, that's how the story was told. I remembered that the girl involved had once been described to me as easy, and I quietly bent the corners of a beermat with my fingers as they all spoke, thinking: *could that happen to me?* As I sat in front of a glass of wine that could strip paint, I wondered, what was the difference between me and the girl who was probably sat in her room crying? A question I presumably only asked myself because I already knew the answer – there was no difference. We were as vulnerable as each other.

Later on, the girl came to the pub. I remember her looking completely nonplussed, just having a normal afternoon drink. I remember thinking: *why are you here? Their friends tried to rape you.* That evening passed, that week passed, and everybody moved on. I don't know whether their behaviour was ever reported. I can only remember the name of one of the boys, and one rainy afternoon nearly a decade later, I look him up on LinkedIn. From his top private school and his top university, he has gone on to a top job invariably making lots of money. What is scary is that none of those top-brass settings gave him the education or wherewithal to think twice about doing a Houdini. But what is even scarier is that one day he'll be able to send his own son through the exact same route.

*

We all know a story like that; it might not be the Houdini, but it will be a moment of egregious sexual ignorance and boundary-crossing that sends a chill up our spine whenever we revisit it. In the past ten years, campaigns such as Everyday Sexism, #MeToo and Everyone's Invited have created space for young people to share their experiences of rape culture.

The world feels like it's becoming better, like a big, cultural zit has finally been squeezed. But the problem is that zits leave an open red sore that needs to heal. Or they simply return, bigger than before.

Academics like Katherine Angel have labelled this era 'the age of consent'. In my own short lifetime, interest in consent has grown exponentially from the 2017 turbo-boost of the #MeToo moment. In *Hansard*, the official report of all Parliamentary debates, the usage of the term 'sexual consent' has increased consistently since the early 2010s. In the last few years, references in English-language books to 'sexual consent' have overtaken references to 'breadmaking'. Talking about consent has suddenly felt urgent, when in reality, that's exactly what it's always been.

We have always liked reading about sex; in fact, the word's occurrence in the *New York Times* between 1970 and 2018 shows a stratospheric rise, in an almost direct contrast to the number of mentions of 'church'. Loosening social mores has meant we can talk about sex more openly because most of us are having it more openly too – but those conversations did not rise in parallel with discussion about sexual consent. It's as though there's been a time lag: a delayed realisation that, as sexual liberation stretched out its arms, sexual *ethics* sat twiddling its thumbs in the cultural psyche.

Reflecting on my school years, I don't remember ever being explicitly taught about consent, which either means that it was so dull that it made no impact on me, or that it was wholly absent. One of my friends thinks she can remember being told when to say yes and no, but can't remember what the qualifying criteria were. What I do know is that it has always sounded scary. There is something jargonistic about the word consent. Because of its connection to ideas such as the age of consent, rape and sexual assault, the mere mention of the word summons imagery of crime and punishment – of rights being abused, rather than upheld. When pressed to think about it, it makes us think more about what we *can't* do, rather than what we can. One social scientist tells me that sex education in the UK has moved from moral abstinence messaging to anti-teenage pregnancy messaging and now onto consent messaging; it is a long history of can'ts, not cans. And the upshot of all this is that I've had to learn about the realities of consent myself – the hard way.

I learned it the hard way writing this book and encountering the word 'consent withdrawal' for the first time. I realised, ten years later, that my failed attempt to have first-time sex with someone who had no condom and didn't pick up on my unspoken doubt largely happened because I didn't know the concept of consent withdrawal. Giving consent had been presented as a single moment, which I had already cashed in – I had no idea that it could span a whole series of moments in which I'd have the opportunity to withdraw. I didn't know how to verbalise my doubt; instead, I was left with the sense that 'I'm here now, I've made my bed. Now I should sleep in it.' I'd go on to behave similarly in future scenarios, accepting male power as an unchallengeable given and maybe even seeking it out. I should have been taught less about saying outright no, and more about how to know what I want, ask for it, and be prepared to make new choices if I was denied it.

There are many occasions in my sexual biography where I gave my consent at the time, but the details suddenly and dramatically changed – like when a partner disclosed he'd lied about his age, or was breaking up with me, during or after sexual contact. Or what of the times I consented to certain touches or acts, but not others – yet my acceptance of one was taken as an implicit acceptance of the other, and what I took for being *persuaded* I now feel was me being *coerced*? They are all sexual encounters in which, had I known the full truth, I would never have engaged in the first place. The murkiness around all this, and the resilience that I would need to cultivate, were never talked about at school. For most people, they are still not talked about. And that is something we should find terrifying.

*

One of the biggest sex myths today is that consent relates to one area of sex: sex itself, and saying yes or no. We are told that consent is a word that will liberate us from rape and assault – but in reality, it is a red herring. Consent, and the exploiting or desecrating of it, appear far more frequently in our day to day lives and relationships. You gave your consent to send that nude. You gave your consent for your partner to open the door to you, look your body up and down and declare, 'Phwoar!' But you didn't give your consent for that nude to get uploaded to Twitter. You didn't give consent for the STI whose symptoms you noticed a week later, even though they'd said they'd been tested. You didn't give your consent to the man who, when you were en route to your partner's house, gave you the once-over and urged, 'Give us a smile, love!' It's not simply consent that is lacking in many of our day-to-day lives – it's the recognition of our selfhood and agency. Understanding why so many of us are denied this basic right, and introducing and challenging the social scripts around power and gender that trap so many of us in these grim interactions in the first place would teach consent implicitly. Radically, our sex education might not even have to focus on consent in the first place if it did better at guiding young people to recognise the bad ethics of sex *before* they had a chance to mindlessly perform them.

Centring consent in our conversations around sex is like centring possession-owning in our daily life. 'Not getting mugged' is the absolute bare minimum we should expect walking around our cities. But there are other acts that we hold dear: giving things we own or have made to loved ones, and acknowledging when such thoughtful gifts are received. Being able to buy things we deserve and need; being able to buy a treat without guilt. Having things returned to us when we have graciously allowed them to be borrowed. Not having our possessions mocked or broken, be it malevolently or simply as collateral damage. And yet, 'not being raped' is still what sex education and mass media offer when they talk to us about good examples of consent. We deserve so much more – and our wellbeing and public health depend on it.

Preparing ourselves for happy, healthy sex is so much more than learning when to say yes or no. We need the power to eschew all the myths we've been taught and the social scripts we've absorbed, and the resilience and self-esteem to enter what is an exhilarating, sometimes humiliating, uncompromising world of romance.

*

It's been a while since I attended a sex ed class, but here I am, aged twenty-seven, sitting on the floor watching one. The beauty of the pandemic is that I can access this, an hour-long workshop intended for fourteen- to eighteen-year-olds, from the comfort of my living room. Not that I am here to learn about anything comforting, mind you.

The workshop is specifically on consent, and it quickly becomes clear that I am not here to learn how to have a good time. Almost straight away, I am shown a slide stating 'the legal bit', its broad red graphics telling me the age of sexual consent, the age at which I could legally sext and the age at which I could watch pornography – the implication being that this age group isn't old enough to do any or most of it. The big red arrows tell me and everyone else watching that these are all Big Bad Law things, and that I would get into correspondingly big trouble if I did anything of this nature.

Pornography is particularly vilified, with an even bigger red arrow announcing that 42 per cent of fifteen- to sixteen-year-olds have said porn gave them ideas of sexual practices they wanted to emulate. It occurred to me that not all sexual practices in porn are necessarily bad, but that seemed by the by for those delivering the workshop. It quoted an anonymous female, aged thirteen, saying: 'It can make a boy not look for love, just look for sex, and it can pressure us girls to act and look and behave in a certain way before we might be ready for it.' Porn pressurises boys too – and people of all sexualities – but none of these perspectives were offered. So anyone watching would have thought about how bad porn is for girls, how it is watched by boys, and only how straight-couple dynamics might be affected by it. They'd also think that all porn was the same, and bad, and wouldn't learn that its purpose is adult entertainment, for adults, if they want it – which they are not, *yet*. It isn't even supposed to be sex education for adults, never mind young people; porn promises fantastical scenarios, not learning or training. In the new RSE (Relationships and Sex Education) guidance from the government, such sessions are supposed to be more inclusive of LGBTQIA relationships. I'd go a step further: where's the discussion of power and gender?

A lot of the talk was pure legalese, unpicking a definition of consent that made no sense to me, but then didn't make much sense after it was explained to me, either: 'if he agrees by choice, and has the freedom and capacity to make that choice'. Here, the male neutral 'he' employed by English law sounds especially dissonant. It's a school workshop, not a court case – why not explain it in simpler terms for children to understand, and in gender-neutral terms too? According to the session facilitator, a person's freedom could be affected by anything from force to manipulation, intimidation to emotional abuse, and a person's capacity could be affected by their age, special education needs and alcohol intake. Then came more and more lists, one about the different types of exploitation, then another about the signs of exploitation. There were over eleven signs. I finished the Zoom thinking that there were too many lists of things to remember, and that everything was red and bad and telling me not only not to have sex, but that I could very easily be a victim of sexual assault and needed to be on constant high alert. None of the lists had told me how I might actually spot some of these things. What actually qualified as emotional abuse? How much alcohol was too much alcohol? I thought back to my own sex education that was devoid of consent but also full of fear-mongering. I tried to imagine myself as a seventeen-year-old again watching this, someone who already had too many anxieties and myths about the sexual world in her head. I do not think this talk would have calmed her down. The reminder that it was men who committed rape and men who were influenced by pornography would have also reinforced the idea that it was men who did sex; when I had sex, it would be done *to* me.

I spoke to a young woman in Year 12 who told me something similar. Her school was caught up in the 2021 rape-culture scandal over UK schools and universities. She told me that her class were given a consent session specific-ally because their school had been named as part of the investigation into sexual harassment.

'The first line of the lesson was that "cases of sexual assault or rape are often the outcome of a string of bad choices",' she told me. 'The first two options we were given were both about the victim being better at controlling themselves – and when we did tasks they were just about "the law". They showed us the ONS statistics rather than us having an actual discussion about it.'

When we criticise sex education programmes, many of our criticisms lie with abstinence-only or moralistic sex edu-cation; we forget that perfectly secular sex education also comes with its own moral world view. If it terrifies young people, then that, too, is sex-negative teaching. Secondly, it can wildly ignore cultural nuances. Another friend of mine who is a similar age to me remembers being given 'drunk glasses', which have lenses in to distort your vision, and then being asked to put a condom on a banana. The point was to try to tell young women that they were incapable of making decisions if they were inebriated, but there's a catch here. One is that it emphasised to all those girls that it was their job to try to protect themselves, as opposed to it being a conversation between two people. And secondly, that this was a school where most of the pupils were Muslim – non-alcohol drinkers, and many of them unlikely to engage in sex that wasn't marital. Were they ever given sex ed that prepared them for consent awareness over long periods, such as in a marriage?

These aren't the only clangers. A sex education campaign video, paid for by the Australian government for the princely sum of $3.8 million, had to be pulled because of widespread criticism; one TV journalist described it on air as 'six minutes of WTF'. It includes such gems as a woman smearing milkshake on a man's face and telling him to drink it, and a girl being scared to swim at the beach because she's worried about sharks. Why not just . . . mention the word sex? Teenagers know sex happens – why are we pretending that we still can't talk about real scenarios? Fictional people can and should be used in examples to imagine possible situations, but why is actual experience still so unpalatable to educators?

Across UK schools and universities, many students get shown an infamous 'tea' video, where the analogy of trying to make someone drink a cup of tea is supposed to demonstrate when it is and is not okay to try to get someone to have sex with you. 'Consent is like a cup of tea,' it claims, and then explains how if someone is unconscious, but said earlier that they wanted tea, don't give them any tea. Or if they say that they don't want tea, don't give them any tea. In the real world, when do conversations or thought processes about sex ever follow that template? What aspect of that video teaches young people how to navigate and evaluate consent – not only their partner's, but their own?

Sex educators and researchers working in the UK repeatedly cite the video to me as an example of poor consent teaching. An academic paper addressing it published in *Children and Society* in 2019 notes that 'the central "risk avoidance" message of such resources individualises the potential risks of non-consensual sex and ignores the gendered social structures that shape interpersonal relationships'. They add: '[C]onversations with young people are important, but they need to address the complexity of sexual consent, coercion and gendered sexual norms.' This paper has been resoundingly ignored; the video stands at 9 million views on YouTube. One educator I spoke to said to me: 'If you only have a student for a few moments before their first Freshers' night out, is the tea video a good idea? Probably. But only for that night. You aren't preparing them for the future.'

Instead of simplifying how we talk about consent, argue the paper's authors, we need to complicate it. 'The resource reduces the chance of having a conversation about sexual consent as it implies that it is so simple to understand it does not need any discussion, anyone can understand that you don't force tea on a person.' Instead of opening up a conversation around the social norms or cultural context at play, they don't even mention them. That's as good as perpetuating them.

So that's what I'm now going to do. I'm about to make things complicated.

*

'Like I've been saying in the webinars,' says the disembodied voice, 'I've been trying to game the eights and nines.' The man, a radio phone-in caller, has just been speaking about a Filipina woman he went on a date with. 'We met at 9:30. She was there a few minutes later, and she called me to see where I was at, and then *boom*. It was one of those rare occasions where she was better looking in person – a solid 8.5.' Two men, both involved in a YouTube live stream, sit and listen thoughtfully.

The voice continues. 'She started showing the signs. Very giggly. Very feminine. She was preening. She was showing off her neck. And then she started to play with her straw and go back and forth from that to playing with the sleeve on her cuff. And I was like, wow, this is in the bag.'

Much like David Attenborough describing a mating ritual in the Serengeti, this young dater had been analysing every moment of his date. The story goes on. He invites her to his for Netflix and she keeps giggling. 'Pretty much the entire time, she was touching me. And then I went to touch her back and for the first time she started to show a little bit of resistance.' Long story short, she left. 'For the first time since I arrived in this country, I didn't have sex on the first date. So I'm not sure what happened. I'm wondering what to do next. I've gotten so used to nexting girls but this eight or nine girl is a dime.'

Troy Francis, one of the live streamers and a Brit whose social media presence revolves around giving men dating advice, asks if he tried to make out with her. 'I don't get the sense he was pushing the envelope. Did he just allow her to leave? Not that he should force her not to leave – could he not have rolled off a bit? Asked to just chill, and then tried again? Sometimes you need to allow her to feel comfortable.'

The internet hosts dozens of articles and YouTube videos just like this on how to combat LMR – 'last-minute resistance'. It is part of the lexicon of pickup artists, an online community that has been connected by researchers to misogynistic online spaces such as inceldom, men's rights activism and MGTOW (Men Going Their Own Way). Many of them, like the caller in this video, scrutinise and study female behaviour in the pursuit of sex, because they believe that women show certain signs when they are interested. Pickup artistry as an industry has been valued at $100 million, and a growing world of male influencers are populating a thriving speaker market around it.

Laura Bates has written about pickup artistry extensively. 'Like the incelosphere, there are so many sites, forums and message boards, all spewing the same sexist pickup ideology, that it is easy to become quickly desensitised to the skewed portrait of relationships they portray.' She says that many of these resources 'teach (with copious pseudo-academic biological reasoning, of course) that a woman who decides she doesn't want to have sex with a man is not making a rational or valid personal choice, but rather responding helplessly to a biological imperative. Her body, pickup gurus insist, is trained to panic instinctively to avoid sex, in case she dies during childbirth or is abandoned by the father of her children. Yes, really.'

As well as LMR, another popular phrase is ASD – 'anti-slut defences', which may be deployed by women again in an attempt to thwart sex. On Reddit, I find a thread in which some men discuss ASD. A user asks for advice about a girl who, after making out with him, declined to go any further and said, 'I don't want to be the rebound.' Someone replies:

> Girls have a certain 'logic' in their pretty little heads
> about shit like this. The only way to short circuit
> this is for her to be ok with the 'no strings attached'
> arrangement. In other words, if she really wants to
> bang but is afraid to be a rebound, then take the
> possibility of a relationship off the table and let her
> know this is a booty call and nothing more. This
> reverse psychology will help them decide it's OK
> to fuck because she is not going to be the 'rebound'.
> Then her hamster will start running and wonder,

'Wait, why doesn't he want to have a relationship with me?'

Another user suggests that the forlorn lover employs the 'agree and amplify' techniques, which will 'make her look ridiculous', and recommends that he practises them in front of a mirror until they are second nature, emulating the energy and delivery of an actor or 'alpha' male they admire. He tells him to say, 'Are you implying I only want you for your body?' and to 'squeeze/slap her ass and laugh then pull her head back and go straight for her neck'. Then he suggests adopting another technique, which he calls the 'Master-Daddy/Student-Girl energy'. 'Stop kissing and grab her chin with your hand and stare deep into her eyes like it's a scene from a movie. Lower your voice and say: "Name . . . listen to me . . .*pause* . . . stop acting like a fucking twelve-year-old." Immediately break into a smile/laugh to break some tension and playfully slap her cheek and wag a finger in a face like you're her dad. Then significantly spike her arousal by escalating sexually. Really squeeze her ass/tits/hips, pull her on top of you, pull her head back and go for her neck."

Believing that women don't know what it is that they want, secretly want something they are biologically conditioned to avoid, or that they are stupid enough to be gamed are views that need to be discussed and dismantled when young people are still at school. Literature around desire, agency and healthy relationships needs to actively debunk some of these ideas that proliferate online and in the school corridors, as this is where non-consensual notions of persuasion and gaming are allowed to thrive; hostile sexism is something that needs to be challenged, not ignored.

Opportunistic sex in the vein that many of the men describe in these forums doesn't *have* to be inequitable; two randy work colleagues taking advantage of an empty office might be breaking some of their employer's rules, but if they are both consenting adults, the problem is at least not consent. But in cases where partners do not feel like they give their consent, or where they make it clear they want to go more slowly or change direction, we need to interrogate why there is no equity in those moments – not only of consent, but also often respect and pleasure. Addressing these things often demands that we speak more candidly about the mechanics of sex – so often avoided in 'proper' discussion or sex ed – which would better prepare young people to spot incursions into their agency.

It's not only a conversation that's urgently needed for women, but for members of the LGBTQIA community too, as well as the minority of men who are abused by female perpetrators. There is a lack of research on both, despite the charity SurvivorsUK finding in 2021 that nearly half of gay and bisexual men in Britain have been sexually assaulted. A review of literature on sexual-assault-perpetrator characteristics that I find from 2015 repeatedly refers to a *lack* of literature, though there are a few leads. In one study among members of the armed forces, 34 per cent of victimised men felt the incident was a form of hazing, an act of humiliation.

In research from the Nineties, two groups are identified as committing assault against men: homosexual men committing it for intimacy and sexual gratification, and heterosexual men committing it as an expression of social dominance or control. Victims of harassment and assault would be the first to tell you that rape is not the only scenario in which they feel like others have tried to control, dominate or use them for gratification; from homophobic slurs to non-consensual touching in bars, the micro-aggressions of assault are felt here too. We only have to think back to Quinn, from Chapter 4, who was made to question a profound sexual moment, on the grounds that it wasn't 'proper sex' – exactly the kind of coercive framing that would force someone into having anal sex when they didn't want to. Why aren't we better equipped to talk about these moments too, as well as rape? The same literature review found that female perpetrators of crimes involving male victims were also perfectly capable of coercion, namely behaviours designed to induce arousal and emotional manipulation like threatening a break-up. Centring consent here feels futile when what needs to be centred is control, and its abuse; why do so many seek to exert it over other people?

We are getting better at talking about normalised coercion, albeit usually through a heterosexual lens. One of the nastier examples of this is stealthing. Forget the 'consent is like a cup of tea' video; Michaela Coel's *I May Destroy You* has been far more responsible for opening up a nuanced conversation about *conditional* consent, which is when ostensible consent to intercourse is then broken because certain conditions have been violated. In it, Michaela's character is consensually having sex with someone with a condom, but he then removes the condom without her noticing. Here, the man has wholly ignored the risk to his partner's health, the right to bodily autonomy and, worst of all, the risk of pregnancy. But because she consented to sex, the removal of a condom is somehow seen as insignificant. Has the gravity of inequity – that the risk is hers to bear, not his – really weighed on him? Or has he simply seized on a moment?

Lots of people don't like wearing condoms, but that's not the point here; an alternative method of contraception might have been discussed if that was the case. But if that was the reason he didn't want to wear a condom, then he put his pleasure before hers – because how can you have pleasurable sex if it isn't consensual?

The *Independent* interviewed a man who claimed to stealth, who said: 'I'd be more worried about getting an STI than getting someone pull a lawyer on me for fraud when I'm having sex and I take a condom off.' Fraud!? It's rape! Lots of people don't seem to think it's rape. There are campaigns in numerous countries trying to criminalise stealthing – that's how many people don't think it's rape. If it were truly seen as rape, a law wouldn't need to be created because *it is already illegal to rape someone.*

Not nearly enough research has been done on why some men behave in this way. There is one disturbing but small study that was published in the *British Medical Journal* in

2016, which interviewed fifty-one men and found that they were more likely not to want to use a condom with someone they considered attractive. On top of that, the more attractive a participant judged himself to be, the more he believed that other men like him would engage in condomless sex and the less likely he was to use a condom himself. Another study, from the *Journal of Health Communication* in 2019, also found that more frequent pornography consumption was associated with using condoms less *if* the man considered porn to be his primary source of information about sex. If porn wasn't their primary source, their rate of condom use was unrelated to their porn consumption. If young people don't realise stealthing is rape, it's very possible they also don't understand the socially conditioned decisions they are making behind these acts in the first place, above all when they are normalised. In 2020, a viral rap called 'body 2' featured the lyrics, 'Have you seen the state of her body? If I beat it, I ain't wearing a johnny'. This specific section was amplified as a trend on TikTok, where millions of young people who'd never even had sex yet lip-synced to its lyrics.

Researchers have spotted a similar normalisation of other coercive acts, including anal hetero sex. A 2014 paper in the *British Medical Journal* found that there was an acceptance of female reluctance and expectations of pain for women, but, despite that, an equal acceptance of coercion. 'Even in otherwise seemingly communicative and caring partnerships, some men seemed to push to have anal sex with their reluctant partner despite believing it likely to hurt her,' they write. Women seemed to take for granted that they would 'either acquiesce or resist their partners' repeated requests' for anal sex, 'rather than being equal partners in sexual decision-making'. Several respondents confessed to 'slips' where anal penetration had been accidental, and the researchers explain that while the data is poor on whether these *are* actually accidental or not, one of their respondents changed his testimony during the course of interviews. 'I tried, and I said it slipped,' he eventually said, confessing to slyly attempting anal sex without first seeking his girl-friend's permission.

If we look more widely at other studies, we might also better understand where consent and access to equitable sex is ignored if we understand why certain people hold a lack of empathy for women. The anal hetero sex study intim-ated that the desire to compete with other men essentially overrides any sensitivity towards their partner. Other studies point to further empathy-killers, such as women dressing 'provocatively'. One study in 2009 found that some men were more likely to objectify women who wore fewer clothes compared to those who wore more clothes, but not all men; specifically the participants who had 'high hostile sexism scores'. These scores highlight men who hold views like 'women are controlling' or 'invading male public space'. They were quicker to associate sexualised, bikini-wearing women with first-person action verbs – 'I push, I grasp, I handle' – and clothed women with third-person action verbs – 'she pushes, she grasps and she handles'; so they saw agency in the more clothed women, and objects in the less clothed ones. Female participants, irrespective of whatever hostile sexism scores they had, did not demonstrate the same pattern as the men. The study also found that higher hostile sexism scores in men predicted a decreased activation of the part of their brain that helps them 'mentalise', a psychological term describing how we make sense of other people and their mental states. In other words, empathy. Are these attitudes addressed in sex education – and if they aren't, what happens if you don't teach men about the power society has historically granted them, but do teach them that victims are likely to get into sticky situations after 'a string of bad choices', and essentially only have themselves to blame?

As well as a lack of empathy, these 'high hostile sexism scores' are at the root of other consent-ignoring problems in society. A 2021 study published in *Psychology and Sexuality* sought to investigate the drivers behind catcalling in men. It found that men who were reported to have catcalled demonstrated higher levels of hostile sexism, self-ascribed masculinity and 'social dominance orientation'. So when men and women insist 'not all men' online, they are right. It isn't all men. But it is men with high hostile sexism scores, who are eager to perform it without realising what it could be revealing. And there are a lot of them.

Lastly – and this brings us back to the idea of inequitable sex – lots of men think that this kind of behaviour will actually get them sex, demonstrating a gross misunderstanding of what it is women want. Canadian researchers in 2019 found that 44 per cent of the men they interviewed who had sent a dick pic had done so in the hope of receiving a photo in return, and 33 per cent thought they'd be able to find a sexual or romantic partner from it. Only 18 per cent saw it as a means of personal gratification. One in ten conceded it was a way of exerting power and control, and – surprise, surprise – men who sent these pictures scored more highly on the hostile sexism score. Numerous campaigns are calling this kind of behaviour cyber flashing, but is that what is really going on here? Those results don't suggest this is exhibitionism; they suggest it is open, unabashed sexual solicitation. They don't intend on a quick flash, and scuttling away. They intend on penetrating you.

You want to sort the world's consent problem? You can create as many laws and fund as many safety programmes as you like; you can make a light-hearted video about tea and you can ensure that consent is included in the national curriculum. But if you don't find a way to talk frankly about normalised coercion, to lower hostile sexism scores and to relieve men from the world view that they must seek control, these problems will likely never disappear. Fixing the 'consent' problem will require alternative vocabulary about power and control: who gets it, how to use it and how to hold everyone who has it – even those you must love and trust – to account.

*

Flick remembers her school – 'a pretty bog-standard UK secondary school in the Nineties' – as never mentioning the word consent. She remembered that the focus of the lessons was not to get pregnant and not get an STI, the consequences of which she was shown in vivid photographs of seeping genital warts. Her teacher instructed the class to roll condoms down plastic models they had been handed – and so Flick ended up having no trouble telling her future male partners to put a condom on, or assisting herself. What she did have trouble with was knowing how to say what she wanted. Nor did she know how to say no – because she didn't realise that she could say no in the first place.

'I had no idea what a healthy, mutually fulfilling sexual relationship looked like,' she explains. For 'most of my twenties and early thirties, I felt that you basically had to agree to what guys wanted to do in bed, whether you really wanted to do it or not'.

If you are lucky enough to be at school now or have children at school, they should be getting the new Relationships and Sex Education curriculum that has recently been introduced in England. Between eleven and sixteen, children gradually learn about the laws around consent in a safe classroom environment as well as the laws around sharing sexual images and porn, and explore trust and vulnerability. The guidance from the PSHE Association advises that teachers introduce consent, then talk about the law and avoiding assumptions, the right to withdraw consent, the capacity to consent in the first place, and then finally coercion, sexual images, rape myths and victim blaming. Those last three lessons, it emphasises, are aimed to support pupils thirteen and older.

It sounds quite good – but in reality, how young people are taught about consent still suffers from enormous resourcing problems. Training in this new RSE curriculum has been shockingly low; in September 2021, the Minister for School Standards admitted that four out of five schools still had not received the mandatory training to teach it. It was not the first government to have been challenged on this, and neither was it the first time that the minister explained the 'cascade' modelling of schools, in which only a few are given training with the expectation they will go on to train other schools in their area. He also added that Department of Education training modules are available to download for free, anyway. Wondering if schools were actually listening to him, I filed a freedom of information request to find out how many times the training module that covers consent in secondary schools had been downloaded – 1,775, as of October 2021. There are 3,456 secondary schools in the country, which doesn't count independent senior schools, of which England has the highest proportion in the UK. So we can assume that not even half of English senior schools are teaching up-to-date consent classes.

Even in the schools where this curriculum *is* taught, there are signs that it's coming too late. If most children have been exposed to porn by age eleven, why do they have to wait until they're nearly at key stage 4 to find out how it connects to their own bodies and self-image? One woman, Lucy, is now twenty-one, and had her first lesson on consent in Year 12. But by that point, she had already been coerced into sending a boy a nude because she didn't understand that she could say no to him. 'Make people take a sexual health and relationships GCSE,' she told me. 'They could actually teach about female pleasure, consent, masturbation and all kinds of sex, instead of teaching girls how not to get pregnant and normalising male-only pleasure.'

Parents can still withdraw pupils under sixteen, meaning they would miss out on elements of sex education entirely (but not relationships or health education). What's more, faith schools are still allowed to carve out elements of the curriculum, adapting them to their religion's social teaching.

The track record for faith schools on this count is bleak. Someone who left a Catholic school in Essex the same year I left school had the sex education chapters ripped out of their school textbooks in Years 7 and 8, and throughout school had to respect a six-inch rule between boys and girls. A pupil at an all-girls' Church of England school tells me that her class were taught to put condoms on courgettes, but that the Catholic boys' school across the road never did. So if any of those boys or girls ever met each other, the onus of condom-applying was going to be on the girls. Another girl told me her school's sex education was so vague that she didn't realise that men ejaculate when they orgasm.

In her book *Tomorrow Sex Will Be Good Again*, academic Katherine Angel pokes numerous holes in our understanding of consent, as well as our obsession with it in the twenty-first century. She believes that 'the widespread rhetoric claiming that consent is the locus for transforming the ills of our sexual culture' is flawed. She asks: 'Are consent, saying yes, and expressing desire a guarantor of pleasure? Do they preclude men's instrumentalization of women? Of course not. Pleasure, and the right to it, are not equally distributed.'

Sex, she says, is an unequal exchange of risks; the idea that an agreement may be made ahead of intercourse implies that there is a sexual imbalance to risk and injury, and that, for some people, sounds like too much work. But work is what is needed.

Sex and relationships will always have collateral damage. Love will always be roses and thorns. But the point is that issues such as consent, ethics and kindness are implicitly woven into the daily interactions we have with everyone who walks into our sex lives and beyond, and we all come to the table with different ideas and experiences of what these concepts mean. It takes us right back to the beginning of this book, where virginity-loss experiences are clearly affected by the different ages and socio-economic, faith, racial, gender and educational backgrounds that we all come from. It is not only first-time sex that is coloured by these many factors, it is *every*-time sex. Recognising those differences and looking for the space to have equitable sex is what will level us – not meagre posturing around consent classes.

In 2021, a group of researchers published a paper in *The Lancet* that argued for sexual wellbeing to be better monitored in public health. They pitched a model for it that holds seven key indicators of sexual wellbeing: sexual safety, sexual respect, sexual self-esteem, resilience in relation to sexual experiences, forgiveness of past sexual experiences, self-determination in your sex life and, finally, comfort with your sexuality. They even suggested ways to measure these: evaluating feelings of safety, acceptance of sexual identity, forgiveness of mistakes, feeling focused and an absence of unwanted thoughts during sex, to name just a few. We could, if we wanted, do better research here, and better data collection. Instead of measuring the rate of STIs, we could be measuring how safe women feel in bed, how confident men feel about their masculinity and sexuality. *That* is the data we need and the conversations we want to start, if we really want to talk about 'consent'.

And that is where the future of our sex lives lies, if we decide we want to do something about this. It needs to look far beyond all the sex myths we have been told about how our sexual history, our bedsheets, our physiology, our peer groups and our sex lives speak for us. We need to learn that we are in control of our bodies, but not in control of the bodies of others; it is a power that comes with responsibility and, above all, empathy. For many of us, that power has never been ours. But here it is, finally – just within arm's reach, if we stretch out far enough.

8

The Future Story of Sex

When Amirah was growing up, her mother told her about periods, but that was it. At school, she can remember being taught about what sex was and how it could make a baby, but it left her with no clue of how to actually do it. All she knew was that, once she was married, it would become acceptable within the parameters of her Muslim faith. Fast forward ten years, and Amirah is talking to me with an easy authority about the mechanics of the pelvic floor.

'I really feel it would be great for girls to practise using dilators,' she says. 'I have a daughter, she's seven, and before she gets married I'm going to try and convince her to use dilators.'

After all my interviews, I am surprised that Amirah, possibly one of the most religious people I have spoken to, says such a thing. But when she looks at her daughter, she sees herself. She sees a little girl who is one day going to become an adult – and if society doesn't change around her, Amirah sees a young woman who may enter her marital bed as clueless, disempowered and in pain as her mother did. 'That's the person that I am,' Amirah says, defiantly. 'She will be confident when she loses her virginity.'

Amirah was barely out of school when she got married and started experiencing pain when she and her husband tried to have sex; it was 2008, and the awareness around vaginismus was even worse than it is now. When the marriage was pushed to breaking point, she googled her symptoms and realised that there was nothing at all wrong with her – it was just a pain condition. 'I bought dilators, and I got to the last size of the dilator,' she explains. 'For most women, they need a combination of dilator therapy, coaching, support – *emotional* support. Some may need deeper psychological support, while for others it's very surface-level.'

For Amirah, a practising Muslim for whom activities like masturbation are prohibited, suggesting that her daughter uses a dilator to familiarise herself with her own anatomy is ground-breaking. It is, however, in line with official guidance; some time after our interview, the National Institute for Health and Care Excellence opened a consultation for new guidelines on the management of pelvic floor dysfunction, and recommended in the draft that young women, aged between 12 and 17, should be taught about pelvic floor anatomy and pelvic floor muscle exercises as part of the school curriculum. It is understandable that someone like Amirah is asking for this as she recognises how little she knew about herself, and all the work that she has had to do to relinquish the sex myths that she had been raised with –

namely, that sex was dirty, and painful for women. Amirah used to be a high school science teacher, but when she made a YouTube video about her experience with vaginismus, more women than she'd ever spoken to in her life reached out to her asking for help. It sparked a career change; she got a certificate as a life coach and, years later, advising women to stop thinking that sex has to be painful and to start thinking about the health and pleasure opportunities that the pelvic floor holds has become her full-time job. Though their faith backgrounds vary, all her clients were raised to believe that 'sex is bad, sex is taboo'.

Many of her clients do not only believe that sex is painful; they have actively been taught that sex is *supposed* to be painful for women. 'I don't know why women are spreading these myths that it's supposed to hurt,' Amirah complains. 'We should all learn how to insert something in a pain-free way. Ninety per cent of my clients currently have vaginismus, and a small minority are not yet married and are worried, or have gotten divorced because of it. Surely, prevention is better than the cure? Women could be taught about it preventatively – at school we could be taught that it's a condition, and that there are methods to prevent it from happening. Sex shouldn't be painful, or scary.'

I have spent whole chapters dispelling sex myths, but ultimately, what's going to replace them? Innovators like Amirah have the answer: new stories that aren't myths. Her story is that sex *isn't* scary or painful and that sex *is* healthy. How does she spread it? She uses social media: smart, clickbait-esque YouTube titles and Instagram DMs to connect with women and bring them into a space where they can be assured of sensitivity and privacy. And how does she back it up? She uses factually accurate information and 3D models of the pelvic floor, but it's more than that; for her predominantly Muslim client base, she grounds this new story in the same world they frequent every day – their faith. 'In Islam, we are rewarded by Allah for having sex with our husbands,' she explains. 'The more you enjoy it, the better. So there is nothing against pleasurable sex. They see it as something that is dirty, because that is what culture has told them. It's not from the religion at all.'

Sex education shouldn't be passive teaching, but the active *un*learning of myths and re-education. In order to do this, you need to tackle the myths head on, rather than simply pretend that they don't exist, and crucially it involves a soft skill in which not everyone gets training: storytelling. The ability to tell and spread change-making stories is what every misinformation crisis lacks, from climate change to COVID-19, in which misleading content travels further and more quickly than the content debunking it. There is also a sex misinformation crisis; it's just so axiomatic and clouded over with other issues that we forget about it. Amirah might not realise it, but she is practising some of the ideas that psychologists recommend we employ in communication to fight inaccurate information, which include things like clickbait parodying and trying to reach audiences on the platforms where they're active. By borrowing from successes in these spaces – where misinformation busters seem to be operating with far more interest than with sexual health – we stand a chance of changing how people think. This is the recipe they suggest: first, you need to know what motivates your audience, and what they already know. You need to confront false information with factual alternatives and frame it in a way that your audience cares about. Then, you highlight solutions, tell stories and leverage the right messengers. None of this is easy work; it needs access to specific tools, contacts and, frustratingly, time.

These are some of the people and strategies who are working hard to tell the new story of sex. Like Amirah, they're already here making a difference, but the question I want to ask is: will their stories and messages reach the people who so desperately need to hear them?

*

Justin Hancock bashfully describes himself as 'just a white bloke from Derby' and probably doesn't realise that because of this very identity, he is a role model for white blokes everywhere: *if Justin did it, you can too*. For years Justin has worked tirelessly to create one of the country's best-known web resources for sex education, called BISH.

A million people from around the world visit BISH every year. Justin has been able to offer and add to the site because of Patreon, a subscription platform for content creators, and at one time also Durex. In the past, his funding came from somewhere very different – a local authority. When he started BISH in 1999, the local authority's youth service had a specialist youth work team, which sent him out to deliver RSE around the city, run sexual health projects for disenfranchised youth and design specialist outreach services. Now, the specialist youth work team is gone, as is the youth service, and many of the people that Justin used to work with have been forced out of the sector altogether. 'The reason I put so much work into this,' he tells me, 'is because when clinics are being closed, and where sex education resources are being denied to young people, and where there isn't enough RSE in the timetable . . . at least this is something they can go to directly.'

In real terms, England's local authority public health budget was cut by £700 million between 2014 and 2015 and 2019 and 2020. As a result, sexual health service budgets were cut by 25 per cent. So instead of the government funding people like Justin, his work is now down to his own loyal fanbase as well as a one-time investment from a multinational condom company. Most people – 55 per cent of them being young men – find his website from googling. These aren't necessarily people who are googling 'BISH'; they're young people who are googling legitimate questions about sex and their bodies, and Justin's web pages are some of the top Google search results. This is partly because Justin clearly understands search engine optimisation, as well as the questions young people are actually curious about; it gives him the freedom to be quite provocative with how he couches material. 'I think bigger organisations, official ones, kind of play it safe. But in playing it safe, I think they often get it wrong. The website is just me. There's no committee, no board of trustees. It's just me.'

He can only spend two days a week on it and would be a lot happier if his site involved a broader range of contributors – hence his declaration of 'just being a white bloke from Derby'. The way that Justin writes is accessible: sex-positive and colloquial, without being patronising. But informed, trained individuals like him are increasingly hard to come by. This is all the more distressing in a country where Ofsted, the government department that inspects schools, found in 2021 that sexual harassment and online sexual abuse had become 'normalised' in schools, with nine in ten girls saying that sexist name-calling and being sent explicit pictures or videos happened 'a lot' or 'sometimes'.

In addition to the usual questions young people have about sex and the body, Justin is seeing an increased appetite for information around consent and thinks that the 'consent is like a cup of tea' resources could be vastly improved. That's why he's pushing for more nuanced lessons around consent and has developed class exercises that help young people understand their sexual autonomy. Such lessons are dramatically different to the ones I had growing up. 'Agency is a word I wish I heard more,' he sighs. 'How do we build our decision-making power, use our power [and understand] how it's unfairly distributed in society?'

One of the exercises he has developed with his colleague Meg-John Barker simply involves getting students to shake

each other's hands. But as the exercise develops, they realise that there's more than one way to greet someone, and
that people's preferences on style of handshake vary: firm,
soft, short or long. He asks them to develop a handshake
that works well for both of them: 'Look for body language,
eye contact, facial expressions.' It's only after this social
experiment that he'll tell the teenagers what sexual consent
is. It's that implicit, ongoing consent young people like
to learn about; not the scary pressures of the law or the
idea that they could be deprived of justice or compassion
because they didn't scream out 'no!' or 'yes!'

'Students like it when consent equips them to notice
what's happening in the moment,' he concluded. 'It's the key
to sex being more pleasurable. Imagine two young people
ordering from a pizza menu, and they've never had pizza
before. How do they decide what pizza they want? How
do they navigate it together? How do we create a frame-
work where it's okay to slow down – no affirmative consent nonsense. This slow folding, unfolding – feeling more
good, less good.'

Justin's book on consent doesn't promote sex-negative
fear-mongering like many school classes do. Legal questions around assault are set against a much wider range of
themes and issues. Such an approach helps young people
realise that their agency and desires are paramount here, and
that it's only once they are equipped to feel in control that
they are prepared for the scenarios in which that control
is challenged.

That we are dependent on Durex and Patreon to keep work like Justin's going is alarming. As well as a failure to raise the critical mass of sex educators, in 2018 only 29 per cent of schools thought that they had the training to deliver the new Relationships and Sex Education (RSE) statutory curriculum and only 10 per cent thought that their existing RSE was of good quality.

Lucy Emmerson, Chief Executive of the Sex Education Forum, told me that more universities could be training people to become sex education teachers to try to raise the number of trained individuals. 'There are a few universities who have made it a specialism,' she explains, 'but they're nervous about laying on a full-time course just to be an RSHE teacher because there may not be a market for it.'

I tell Lucy about the Special Glue speaker, and I say, 'I guess if my school had a full-time RSHE teacher, there probably wouldn't be the need to get an external speaker in, either.'

She nods. 'We need to spot these traders. Schools are open to freebies too. Schools need to be informed about where their biases are so they can avoid these kinds of things – we've got a guide on working with external agencies. Speakers must add value to the school's own managed programme.'

In a national landscape where there is no standardised training and little funding, people who do want to become full-time sex educators have a piecemeal future lying before them – but these are the people who are going to help tell the future stories of sex, and in the most effective way. The top-three preferred sources about sex information for young people, according to the Sex Education Forum, is school, then parents, and then health professionals. School isn't simply where we are most likely to catch people before they make sexual mistakes; it's where young people most trust the information that they're receiving.

Someone who has overcome these hurdles is Demi, who got their training to be a sex educator from acet UK, which they paid for themselves. 'There isn't a one-way route to become a sex educator,' they explain. 'Any kind of organisation can create a syllabus – obviously we'd like to see that change, and for everyone to get the same qualification.' While the charity does have a Christian ethos, Demi was pleased that the course put forward no religious moral value system.

What Demi is doing is quietly revolutionary. They come from a new generation of sex educators: openly queer (identifying as they/she too) and raised in the age of the internet. Demi wouldn't know how to teach sex ed that wasn't inclusive, because they are informed by their own experiences growing up – and now they have the affirmation of a new national curriculum that states that Relationships and Sex Education in England needs to be LGBTQIA inclusive. At the moment, Demi works primarily with SENCO students, which means a lot of her pupils have special educational needs. Dyslexic herself, she knows what it's like to be presented with a diagram and not understand a thing.

'Differentiating helps students feel involved and not isolated, and all your lessons should be differentiated in the classroom.'

When Demi isn't teaching in schools, they are delivering sex education information online to young people who may have already left school as @s3xtheorywithdemi on Instagram. 'I've had my own friends from school tell me, "Wow, you taught me something I didn't know."' I know how they feel. It's a Tuesday night, and Demi's got a cut-up condom, a femidom and a penis candle on her desk. She has just been showing her students how to make a dental dam, a barrier method for performing oral sex on a vulva or anus. She explains how you cut the tip and the bottom of an ordinary condom, and then cut it down the middle, leaving you with a latex square. It is the first time I, a vulva owner, as Demi would describe me, am learning that there is a barrier method that stops STI transmission when performing oral sex on someone with a vulva, or on anuses. All I remember from school is that condoms were recommended for use during penetrative sex.

Dental dams are more commonly used by women who have sex with women, and generally suffer from a lack of availability – so Demi's trick is a clever way of adapting a widely available sexual health tool into one that's harder to find. Though I find a dental dam on an NHS page about lesbian and bisexual sex, it doesn't have its own dedicated page, as femidoms or condoms do. Surely, heterosexual men would benefit from knowing about them too?

In one of their Powerpoints, Demi tells the assembled viewers, who are all watching on Zoom, 'Let's queerify sex.' They pitch two myths that are held about LGBTQIA sex – that vaginal (they emphasise that we actually should use the term vulval) sex doesn't require the use of a barrier method, and that gay men don't need to use condoms – then explain how the need for a condom doesn't disappear along with the risk of pregnancy as the risk of STI transmission remains. Then Demi mentions finger condoms, another kind of barrier method I'd never heard of. 'If you don't use finger condoms, wash your hands before and after any contact.'

The debunks continue. 'Scissoring is not a real thing! It's one of the most common ways queer people with vaginas are shown having sex. The real name for this act is tribbing.' They challenge the notion that lesbian women always use strap-ons when they have sex, and that a man enjoying penetrative anal sex makes him homosexual. Demi's advice for first times – she doesn't use the word virginity at all – is to be open and honest with your partner, talk about protection, ask for advice and be prepared to guide; you can retract your consent and you don't have to fixate on finishing. She also tells students that they should prepare themselves for 'some internal questioning about their genitals [compared] to your own'. Demi takes the time to emphasise this for trans individuals too, who may be navigating a complex world of sexual desire and gender dysphoria simultaneously.

I ask Demi if anyone in their classes ever mentions virginity, and how they phrase first-time sex themselves.

'I personally would not use the term. I'd bring it up if a student was using it to say that we aren't using this term. I wouldn't use the word virgin either – I'd say "individual who has not engaged in sex yet".

'I'd make it very casual, conversational, I'd probably ask for input, if they'd like to participate, on how they feel about first time, whether they feel pressure, also debunk some pressures in literature or in the media. I'd relate it back to them and their understanding of the world currently. I'd then emphasise there isn't this urgency, there isn't this pressure. It can be a magical experience, or it may not be, and most likely it probably won't be. Sex is a learning experience for your whole life.'

*

Painless sex, sex with agency and having sex with any gender are some of the future stories that we will be able to tell our children if we so wish, but what these various sex educators have shown us are glaring gaps in the system that could stop these positive stories getting to young people before sex myths do: a lack of funding, no standardised training, and a chasm between what young people actually want and what is available to them in busy school timetables. The internet offers educators an arena to try to get past these obstacles; Demi is also on Patreon, and sex educators who are savvy enough to go viral will find that they can monetise their online presences. But there is a catch.

'Social media is a great way, but many educators have been hindered by the new terms of service. I have to use three for sex, so I always write "s3x". I can't talk about certain topics. I'm currently restricted – I only get 200 likes on a post because Instagram hides my content. Even Patreon [which] I use. I did a post on the journey of the sperm cell to the egg cell and before I posted it, it gave me a warning saying it could go against its terms of service. It's upsetting. This is the only education they can get hold of, but our own social media won't let us explore that.'

Demi isn't the only one; I have had TikToks that covered academic research on sexual health which have been reported and taken down under 'adult nudity' guidelines. Before and after the videos have been reinstated, they have lost out on vital engagement time where they could have reached more users. 'I'm a believer that I wouldn't be here without Instagram,' Demi declares, 'and I wouldn't know all the things I'd know without Instagram. We're fighting against an algorithm.'

The American gynaecologist Dr Jennifer Gunter struggled to advertise her book *The Vagina Bible* on social media, because posts with the words 'vaginal' or 'vagina' were automatically rejected. On TikTok, she made a video debunking the hymen-virginity myth with a diagram of a female vagina, with pubic hair and a visible hymen in the background. It got taken down, even though it was very clearly a medical diagram – one that we rarely see – being presented by one of the world's most media-friendly gynaecologists. There could have been a young me watching, a seventeen-year-old who knew nothing about the hymen other than the horror show of pain they'd been led to believe it would cause, who would have benefited from Dr Gunter's sex-positive explanation. Dr Gunter appealed the take down and the video was successfully re-uploaded; it's now had over a million views. Several TikTokkers commented wishing that they had learned about this kind of thing in school.

Institutions suffer as well as individuals; London's Vagina Museum has struggled to fundraise on social media for their charity and physical premises in Camden Town because of the same guidelines, and when they recently launched their TikTok account I was at first unable to find them on the platform because their name meant that they couldn't be searched for. These are all people who are trying to tell the story of sex-positive, pleasure-focused and anatomically detailed sex for women, which has been denied to them for centuries. Dr Carolina Are, a researcher in this space as well as a pole dancer, has been hit with the same sexual/adult nudity post blocks and bans for her dancing. 'This goes back to human rights. I wrote a paper reimagining how social media should be run. It's a corporate civic space. A normal corporate company offline still has to follow the law – but if stuff happens to you and your content online, you have no right or say about it. Human rights guidelines and standards are transnational even if a lot of countries end up breaching them. There's at least a guideline.' She added that there are lots of men who do pole dancing too, mostly from a callisthenics background, bare-chested and wearing joggers, whose videos don't get taken down. 'It's female-presenting people and women that bear the brunt of censorship. I wouldn't be surprised if these tech bros see obscenity and sexuality only with women's bodies. A lot of times we receive unsolicited dick pics and nothing gets done about them; it doesn't count as a community guidelines notification and they blur the picture if the user doesn't follow you. When you report them, they see no penises on their public profile and say that that's fine.'

This censorship is also affecting those who work in science and tech. The landscape is already dismal for scientific research when it comes to women's health; there is five times more research into erectile dysfunction than into premenstrual syndrome (PMS), which affects 90 per cent of women. Women didn't even have to be included in clinical trials by law until 1993 in the US, a country that funds and conducts extensive medical research. It's of little surprise that the femtech market – the development of technology targeted at women's healthcare – is growing rapidly. It would be growing faster if more venture capitalists invested in them, but in 2020 only 2.3 per cent of venture capitalist funding went to female-led startups.

It is exhausting for the women who run these startups, see the societal biases against them and turn to social media to try to rally some support – only to be thwarted there too. I spoke to two inventors and colleagues – Liz Klinger of Lioness Health, which makes 'smart vibrators', and Brianna

Rader from the Jukebox app, which texts people sexual wellness tips, and Slutbot, a text service teaching people how to sext – who have faced obstacles in trying to market their products. Keen to support her friend's fun texting idea, Liz signed up to Slutbot, before realising after a while that she wasn't getting any texts. They realised that it was T Mobile, Liz's provider, blocking them. This Content Lock system, automatically set on phones to filter out 'offensive' material, was also locking individuals out of perfectly consensual sexting; in 2010, PinkNews reported that its site was affected by this same lock, even though it has no adult-related content or advertising on its site. Words deemed of a sexual nature also get these companies blocked from advertising on social media. When Liz tries to buy Facebook ads, 'Anything to do with the vagina, or vulva, or clitoris, or pleasure, it's nearly impossible to do anything with it. There was another device addressing people with menopause which didn't go through because it gets misconstrued as porn or adult pleasure. We're just not able to reach our audiences.'

It's especially frustrating when you have a product like Liz's, which is clearly a health product as much as it is a sexual product. Firstly, it shows that a healthy orgasm exhibits a frequency, a rhythmic movement of pelvic floor contractions that has nothing to do with 'tightness': 'about one to two hertz. It's a very fast movement that's hard to do consciously,' she says. Liz's product would help educate women about their health, but because it's a vibrator, it's frequently branded as too horny for social media ads. This is a completely different experience to companies such as Roman or Hims, who have been able to advertise erectile dysfunction pills everywhere from Facebook to TV ads during American football games. They've now been able to go public too.

Brianna feels like companies such as Facebook and Google get to decide what we can access in an internet that is supposed to be an information free-for-all. She remembers one time when she was running two different ads, one for erectile dysfunction and one about unlocking your female pleasure. The erectile ads were fine, but the other wasn't approved. 'I really don't think there's someone sitting in a room that decides "I'll be sexist today! I'll flick this button!" It's just so ingrained in the algorithm.' Brianna also mentions that it can be harder for people like Liz with physical products to sell. 'Because we're virtual, we sometimes sneak through.'

I ask Brianna if she sees a solution, given that these rules are generally in place to protect young people from seeing sex and nudity. 'Facebook has built features in where we can turn those ads off about fertility or having children. They could do the same thing with other categories – it really isn't that hard. We should be able to see ads for vibrators if we seek them out. Another issue is Google – usually when you google something, it stores that info and then when you go to Facebook, you'll get ads on that Google search. But you can't do retargeting based on anything sexual.' What Brianna is saying is that if you're googling a sexual question such as how to address dysfunction, products that are out there to help you can't find you. They don't know that you're looking for them, because they are classed as sexual, not health-related.

But while lots of us are – despite the obstacles – learning from these apps or these freelance sex educators, we are ultimately doing so because our sex education in schools hasn't prepared us well enough. According to the Sex Education Forum, school is the number-one place where young people want to learn information about sex, before their parents and healthcare professionals. So while it's all well and good that there are ways freelancers can get training, and that femtech entrepreneurs are increasingly coming up with fantastic ideas in this space, governments need to work harder to make sure that schools have the training and incentives to deliver high-quality sex education in the first place.

In the UK, Relationships and Sex Education was only made compulsory in schools in a 2017 Royal Assent in Parliament, and was then only implemented in schools from 2021, delayed a year by the coronavirus pandemic. That means that the guidance behind our sex education curriculum had been unchanged since 2000; it was not updated for *20 years*. In that time, the internet transformed our lives, and it will continue to transform them; even when I was at school, which was still only ten years ago, sexting had not become the widespread nightmare it has become today. That it took so long for our curriculums to even acknowledge it is nothing short of dangerous. In another five years, there will be new problems and new technologies piling on top of the other challenges that this book has outlined: the failure to debunk the sex myths society has taught young people, and an unwillingness to go a step further than harm minimisation to teach them about sexual competence or equity.

Schools that don't implement this sex education well enough also need more accountability. As long as these classes remain just that, and not a GCSE or other kind of examination that evaluates students, measuring other areas of school life such as reports of sexual assault and violence becomes more important. That only 6 per cent of schools were able to deliver Ofsted internal reports of sexual assault and violence when asked in 2021 is horrifying, when all the thirty-two schools and colleges visited in a 2021 inspection were found by inspectors to have problems with sexism, rape and assault. Imagine if schools weren't only rated in league tables by the percentage of pupils getting at least five A* to C grades, but also by student wellbeing, including sexual wellbeing? It would knock some of the top independent schools down for starters, going by the Everyone's Invited list. Ofsted inspectors are now being better trained to spot peer-on-peer sexual harassment because of this review – but schoolteachers need that training too.

Which brings us, as always, to money. The Department for Education said it would provide £6 million of funding in 2019 to 2020 for a school support package to cover training and resources for rolling out the new sex ed curriculum. After the remarks of the Ofsted report, the government suggested that it would possibly add more – but whatever it provided has been nowhere near the £60 million that charities believed was actually needed to arm teachers with the right level of training. In Parliament in March 2021, the Department for Education Minister Nick Gibb assured MPs that his department was grant-funding twenty teaching schools to deliver a 'train the trainer/peer support cascade training programme', which would implement the new statutory Relationships and Sex Education curriculum in their respective regions. But schools, again, often need to pay for this training. After a pandemic, how many can afford it themselves? And how many are given the support to squeeze sex education into already overburdened timetables?

Perhaps it's a culture change that is needed too, one that cannot necessarily be bought. Yuri Ohlrichs has been a sexologist and educator for twenty-five years, and now works with Rutgers, the Dutch centre of expertise on sexual and reproductive health. He thinks the country's natural open-mindedness is a fundamental reason behind its success with young people. Dutch schools have been mandated to teach all students sex education, beginning in primary school, since 2012, and it centres sexual development, diversity and assertiveness. Broadly, Dutch teenagers report that their first sexual experiences were positive, well timed and enjoyable, and most Dutch parents accept sex between teenagers once they are old enough, in steady relationships and staying at the family home. But for him, it's more than sexual open-mindedness – it's a general appetite for problem solving.

'It's a historical thing, part of our geography,' he explains. 'We're very small, threatened by the world. Whenever we had to defend our country against the water, all the different communities had to work together. In trade, we could always set our ideological differences apart and negotiate. We make things work. At school, I had a notebook where I wrote my homework, and there were always two ads: one for a pop icon, and one for Rutgers. So from an early age, we knew we could go somewhere confidential and friendly. We practise a politics of pragmatism, and create laws where everyone gets a little bit of what they want. Many other countries have a dual-party system or strong religious background, but not us.'

Our polarisation in the UK, amped up by Brexit, probably does not help us here. But it is also our ongoing cultural fear that teaching young people about sex is going to make them have sex. How much scientific research has to come out that shows this isn't the case, before people believe this? 'We were working with training for a charity in Warwickshire,' Yuri remembers, 'and in the promo video we talk about what masturbation is. This was with children aged eight or nine. They told us they thought best we do not translate this part. They think we're going to stimulate early sexual behaviour – but the more sex ed that you have in early years, the less likely that you'll start before you are old enough. In the Netherlands, the mean age of first sexual intercourse has increased by one and a half years since five years ago. That is not only due to sex ed – but it's interesting.'

*

I have said from the very beginning of this book that I'm no doctor, therapist or educator; but what I am qualified to do is tell stories, and time and again I can see the same systems preventing us from replacing the wrong information with the right. With social media censoring educational or health information, and sex educators struggling to find the resources to reach the number of young people that they'd like to, we've also got to acknowledge that storytelling is now in a period of constant flux. Every few months, there are algorithmic changes to social feeds that good storytellers need the time and knowledge to stay on top of. We've also got a higher critical mass of storytellers than ever before; that they are more diverse is a good thing, but that they are all trying to compete at once for your eyes in an unforgiving attention economy is a hurdle that only the best resourced can leapfrog. Conventional news sources still misunderstand the mystery of social media feeds, leaving room for creators and educators who haven't always done the same scrupulous research and fact-checking to populate them instead.

Putting life-changing stories in front of the people who are most at risk should form one part of a multi-pronged strategy. Of course we need to see the stories featured more in reputable news outlets, Wikipedia, books and cinema.

But we need to make sure that they're in the quieter, sub-terranean information resources too. They also need to be in the Facebook groups where women are asking about hymen repair; the Instagram resources for asexuals who feel like no one understands them; the forums where young men feel like women are unfairly withholding sex from them. All that takes more than trusted and educated information holders simply knowing how to go viral or tell a good story; it takes a generosity of spirit and the resilience needed to read through the trauma of strangers.

It also isn't just about helping others – it's about helping ourselves. I have had so many moving conversations, almost always with women, about life lessons learned and the new stories that are a balm to sex myths and the unhappiness they have caused. One recent graduate told me that she was raped at a university party, too drunk to have remembered much, but she does remember telling the man she didn't want to have sex, and his worry afterwards when he asked her, 'We're still friends, right?' It was her first experience of penetrative sex, and she was left feeling traumatised and lost, like she had been robbed – though she also shrugged it off as the normal experience of college students, as she had seen in films. Years later, she's had a lot to think about. 'I've realised that my understanding of sex was super hetero-normative,' she says, 'and I placed so much emphasis on penetrative sex even though I had sexual experiences in the past. I now believe my first time was with my high school boyfriend, who I did love. I found a lot of comfort in that.'

I find comfort in retelling my sexual history, and in shifting my language. I don't think the word 'virginity' is going to disappear any time soon, but adjusting how we talk about first-time experiences marks the beginning of a transformative linguistic change that we can all harness in our day-to-day lives. We might think twice before making a sexist joke, or before asking someone if they are dating anybody; before we tell a girl that she's tight, and before we ask someone for their body count. For those of us to whom sex education didn't teach these things, it's incumbent on us to do some of the 'learning' work as adults. But for the young people of today, school remains the most important source of sex-positive information they have access to and is ultimately where their ideas around sex can be formed for the better, so that they'll never have any unlearning to do at all.

And it turns out that in Sweden it's already working.

In 2009, the Swedish Association for Sexuality Education decided that a certain word in the Swedish language was particularly problematic; their word for hymen, *mödomshinna*, literally means 'virginity membrane', enshrining the myth that a hymen defines a woman's sexual history into the language. They came up with a new word – *slidkrans*, meaning 'vaginal corona' – and started using it everywhere: pamphlets from sexual health services, newspapers, Sweden's official language planning body and in all the Association's future communications. They even translated it into the languages of Sweden's largest immigrant communities.

215

Almost ten years later, language planners reviewed how successful the word change had been, and it was huge: 86 per cent of surveyed health professionals had used the word in clinics and class visits. While only 22 per cent of young people had heard of it, more were showing signs of viewing the hymen in a non-traditional way than a traditionally patriarchal one, and many who didn't necessarily use the new word were still parroting the sex-positive phraseology from the Association's pamphlets. Language planning doesn't happen overnight, but it's a start; plus, of the few that did know the new word, a majority described *mödomshinna* as 'a myth'. Others stated simply that 'it does not exist'. And many pointed out that the idea was old or something they'd believed before, in childhood or before someone told them it was a lie. Many other languages around the world, including Czech and Arabic, still call it the virginity membrane – but Sweden has demonstrated that with the right willpower that can change.

Might we need a rebrand in English too? The only etymological reference Wikipedia provides for our word hymen is in its article on Hymen, the Greek god of marriage. 'Derived from the Proto-Indo-European root **syuh, -men-*, "to sew together", hence "joiner" . . . the term hymen was also used for a thin skin or membrane, such as the hymen that covers the vaginal opening.' The hymen does not fully cover the vaginal opening – if it did, a woman couldn't menstruate! It partially covers or surrounds it. Perhaps the crown etymology of 'corona' could make a difference in how we English speakers perceive it too – especially for the 260,000 people who have read that Wikipedia page.

Today's myths will be tomorrow's archaisms, and armed with the right messaging and storytelling, we have never been closer to finally discarding them.

Conclusion:
Nothing to Lose

The envelope sat on my desk for a year, shoved under book piles or used unceremoniously as a coaster, because I wanted to avoid its contents. In it lay my NHS invite to get my first ever cervical screening. I didn't want to go; something inside me knew that, despite years and years of painless sex, my body was still not totally on side.

But as the year passed, that letter grew radioactive. Eventually, the anxiety that I could have cervical cancer outweighed the anxiety over the screening, and I booked my appointment. I lay on the clinical table before a scowling nurse practitioner and breathed out slowly when she started to insert the speculum, but the minute the chilled metal touched my skin, the muscle memory of my apprehension made me spasm. 'Don't do that!' she barked, slapping me on the thigh. I tried not to – I really did.

Still somehow bound to the vaginismus I had hoped was long cured, I realised it's not the only moment in the past year of writing this book that has forced me to reconsider the length and breadth of my own sexual biography. Popular culture bids us to see it simply as a body count and notches on the bedpost. What I hope this book has done is scrutinise the impact and influences of our actions more closely, and instead of seeing one person after the other, I've started instead to see patterns, trauma and, above all, resilience in experiences that were sometimes under my control, and sometimes weren't. I have so often pursued male power, unwittingly ignoring my own. I can see a twenty-seven-year-old man who balanced his pleasure with mine and weighed the scales in his favour – and I can see an eighteen-year-old body wrongly cast as a failure. Really, it was my protector; the invisible force of my pelvic floor was a sign of my strength, not my weakness, as my body tried to tell my brain that it was *mine*, and not *his*.

We probably do not fathom enough how our minds and bodies step in to shield us from an arid landscape of unethical sex. Not a world of bad sex always, but mean sex; unthinking sex. Who knows how our bodies keep this score? Who knows how I bear the generational accumulation of bedsheets being checked for blood and hidden teenage pregnancies in my own family tree? Can barely a generation of sexual freedom tear me away? Can my own life's traumas be eradicated completely – or am I destined to simply cope, every time I get into a bed or go for a check-up? I've learnt that I can be happy, and empowered, and that my resilience is impregnable – but it took finding the right people, and the right information, to get me here. And I remain even more convinced that it could have all been avoided, had I been able to access the right information over a decade ago.

If writing this book has taught me anything, it's that we *don't* live in a world of no information and no research. There certainly will never be enough information or research, but plenty has already been done and made available. My mind was blown reading all the studies I encountered, often expecting a paucity of data but instead finding several, even dozens of papers whose findings on sexual behaviour have never reached someone like me. If you have read anything here and thought, *why didn't anyone tell me that?* then you'll empathise with my writing experience.

When I spoke to a pelvic-floor therapist recently, she told me to complain to the surgery about the nurse who slapped my leg, and to my shame I have not – but that's because I complained somewhere else. I complained in the Department of Health's call for evidence on their Women's Health Strategy in England, where I wrote about all my relevant experiences with healthcare staff over the years. These testimonies will contribute important data to the government's strategy, but it is still incumbent on them to respond to this evidence with action. As I checked box after box that asked if I knew about menstrual wellness, or contraception, or pregnancy, I kept thinking about the litany of things that women have to deal with every day, which men simply do not. Staring at this list, I felt like I finally understood what incels mean when they talk about 'red pill' thinking, taken from *The Matrix* where the red pill reveals the world in the true, gritty reality that is usually obscured to you. But the red pill I've taken seems to have a distinctly different flavour to theirs, which makes them hate themselves, and women. My red pill has just made me realise how limited my access to equitable sex is – and that is me speaking with the privileges of whiteness, private education and a hetero-sexual, cisgender identity. Savour the red pill, and taste how much more limited it is to people from ethnic minorities, LGBTQIA sexualities, and other diverse backgrounds. And – horrifyingly – how limited it also is to young men, who are supposed to be the ones who benefit from the patriarchy in the first place, yet here we all are, screwing ourselves up as much as we are each other.

The irony is that our parents, schools, healthcare systems and governments already think that they are protecting us from harm, obsessing over access to condoms and aware-ness around the age of consent. But we deserve more than the bare minimum. Schools need to do so much better, but so do parents. Research is showing us that mothers are more likely to have conversations about sex with their chil-dren than fathers, and that conversations are more likely to happen with daughters than sons. I think that this shows an implicit understanding, or at least some benevolent sexism, that women need protecting whereas men can do whatever they want, as long as they wear a condom. The idea that women need protecting, today more than ever, is uncom-fortably not wrong – but it's our infrastructure, healthcare services and wider society that need to be taking up the mantle, rather than abandoning women to their fate, or telling them that the best way to protect themselves is to alter their behaviour, rather than power holders themselves attempting to alter men's. Less digitally literate parents who don't have the time to follow lots of websites and social media accounts may still be guided to online courses especially made for them, which do exist. Our parents had appalling sex education, and poorly informed sex lives. In order to protect us, they need to reflect on their own sexual biographies with the learnings of today, while acknowledging the new challenges of the internet, such as sexting and pornography. An understanding of power and gender needs to fill our classrooms, our media and our mindsets – but, above all, our homes.

When I look back at my own life and think of the people who have behaved with the most empathy and kindness when it comes to sex, it is not necessarily the people who had the best access to education or sex education. It's the people who have been encouraged, and not punished, to show vulnerability and altruism. It's the people who have been raised to communicate and express themselves, and not the people who have been told to have a stiff upper lip and get on with it. Even the most sexually awkward and introverted individual can have access to these soft skills – we all can. Even if your child is too young to learn about sex, you can teach them not only about power and gender. You can teach them kindness. And in a book that has criticised sex education programmes around the world, I have also in every chapter told the stories of individuals who have educated themselves, in spite of those programmes. Really, whatever the quality of your sex education, what I hope the mythbusters I have spoken to prove is that the learning journey never ends – what we can hope to access is a comprehensive school education, followed by a fulfilling lifelong education. We learn from every sexual experience that we have, and the many non-sexual experiences that inform us about intimacy, agency and power. It is exhilarating that we never stop learning about sex, and that our bodies change throughout our lives. It gives us every opportunity to be kinder and smarter – and what other life experiences let us do that while having so much fun?

This book began with unravelling the virginity myth, and at its close, I want to return to that. It is where we first begin to understand ourselves and our sexual identities, and if you're reading this, you sit in one of two camps – you have had sex or you have not had sex. Neither of those means you are experienced or inexperienced; competent or incompetent; happy or unhappy. When we lose our virginity, who exactly wins? At the end of this book, I see no victor. And while I respect people's personal decisions to label themselves as virgins, it is a word that I use now with hesitation and clarification. The media's obsession with virginity-loss experiences and labelling people virgins needs to be dismantled. We need to speak about early sexual experiences as exactly that: a set of experiences, a process. You need to tell someone what their body is capable of doing and enjoying, and then you tell them what they can do relationally with others. It is very human of us to label, but this label needs to be used with caution, and in many cases peeled off and chucked in the bin. Once we have done that, the other ideas around penetration, sexlessness and rigid gender roles also begin to collapse – but without hitting the virginity myth hard, disappearing the other myths too could prove impossible.

Virginity and its ancillary myths may linger today, but the clock is ticking on their lifespans. The internet is young, and is providing us with new, interconnected ways to scrutinise and dismantle them. Sure, this is work that will tax us: it will take generations, translations, investment and require many of us to revisit our own traumas so that we can protect tomorrow's youth. But it's clear that this necessary work is already happening; more and more of us are becoming storytellers.

If I have children, I will raise them knowing that, when they're old enough, they'll have a rich life ahead of them. Throughout it, they will have the power to choose the role that sex plays in their lives. Everything is about sex, except sex itself, according to Oscar Wilde; sex, instead, is about power. My children will not be powerless. And they will have no virginity, or anything else for that matter, to lose.

Selected Bibliography

Jonathan A. Allan, Cristina Santos and Adriana Spahr (eds),
  Virgin Envy: The Cultural Insignificance of the Hymen
  (Zed Books, 2016)

Katherine Angel, *Tomorrow Sex Will Be Good Again*
  (Verso, 2021)

Laura Bates, *Men Who Hate Women: The Extremism Nobody
  Is Talking About* (Simon & Schuster UK Ltd, 2020)

Hanne Blank, *Virgin: The Untouched History* (Bloomsbury,
  2007)

Laura M. Carpenter, *Virginity Lost: An Intimate Portrait of
  First Sexual Experiences* (New York University Press, 2005)

David Ghanim, *The Virginity Trap in the Middle East*
  (Palgrave Macmillan, 2015)

Yudit Kornberg Greenberg, *The Body in Religion*
  (Bloomsbury, 2018)

Dr Karen Gurney, *Mind the Gap: The Truth about Desire
  and How to Futureproof Your Sex Life* (Headline Home,
  2020)

Kate Lister, *A Curious History of Sex* (Unbound, 2020)
Laurie Mintz, *Why Orgasm Equality Matters – And How to Get it* (HarperOne, 2017)
Jessica Valenti, *The Purity Myth* (Seal Press, 2010)

Other Reading & Resources

Dr Kirstin R. Mitchell, Catherine H. Mercer, George B. Ploubidis, Kyle G. Jones, Jessica Data, Nigel Field, et al., 'Sexual function in Britain: findings from the third National Sexual Attitudes and Lifestyles' (*The Lancet*, 2013)

Prof. Kirstin R. Mitchell, Ruth Lewis, Prof. Lucia F. O'Sullivan, Prof. J. Dennis Fortenberry, 'What is sexual wellbeing and why does it matter for public health?' (*The Lancet*, 2021)

Love Matters Arabic, an Arabic-language sex education resource: www.lmarabic.com

BISH UK, Justin Hancock's sex education website: www.bishuk.com

The Clit Test, raising the bar for the sex we see on screen: www.theclittest.com

Acknowledgements

First, I would like to thank Grace Pengelly, my editor, who somehow managed to pluck me out of literary obscurity in the middle of a pandemic and gave me the confidence that I was capable of writing a book in the first place. Her editing and guidance throughout this process has made my first book a true joy to write; she never paled or giggled at the idea (as colleagues often have) that sex in society wasn't gratuitous or seedy, but was a potent health and political issue. Similarly, my agent Emma Smith has been immensely supportive and also never balked at the themes of the book, and I would like to thank both the teams at HarperCollins and the Wylie Agency for their faith in me. I am very lucky to have such thoughtful cheerleaders around me. A special shout-out to Katy Archer, Madeleine Feeny, Helen Upton, Matt Clacher and Lindsay Terrell, as well as Paul Erdpresser, Malissa Mistry, Rochelle Dowden-Lord, Jacqui Seagrove and Angela Thomson – not forgetting Emma Pidsley for the lovely jacket.

I am also lucky to have so many curious and inquisitive TikTok followers, many of whom have messaged and interacted with me over the course of writing this book with stories, questions and – most kindly of all – digital pats on the back. They have assured me, with their optimism and intelligence, that we are very much capable of making the world a better place.

This book involved countless interviews and I am so grateful to the many incredible change-makers who took the time out of their taboo-tackling to speak to me, but I would like to offer a special thanks to Dee Hartman, who somehow turned an interview about chronic pelvic floor pain into a real party and who also gave me lots of advice, as well as the sex educators, including Justin Hancock and @sextheorywithdemi, who too often work thanklessly to share their knowledge. I'd also like to thank the many doctors who spoke to me, especially Dr Leila Frodsham, who ever since I made a vaginismus film with her at the BBC has been a warm and generous font of knowledge despite being busy doing a very important job.

Though it has been a few years now, I am indebted to the wonderful modules I had access to while studying Spanish and Arabic at Durham University, and two game-changing professors – Andy Beresford and Abir Hamdar – without whom this book would have been turgid and humourless. The fun yet scholarly rigour they gave to sexuality, literature and the arts in their specialisms was infectious, and is part of the reason why this book is also filled with so many (sometimes bizarre) textual references.

I would like to thank the Gals groupchat, especially Megha Mohan for giving me the crucial advice that good stories need jeopardy. The groupchat has a notable absence, Hanna Yusuf, who I have dedicated this book to. Hanna and I spent hours talking about many of the issues that this book has raised. Her face may be missing at my book launch, and her laughter sadly silenced, but her wish to see a better world for women is one that I clung to in every chapter that I wrote.

I owe a huge debt of gratitude to Luke, my partner in crime and my boyfriend, for his copyediting but especially his patience and perseverance with a girlfriend who, very early in our relationship, started asking him lots of sex questions because she claimed she was 'writing a book about it'. He answered honestly and candidly every time.

Lastly, I would like to thank my parents.

A big thank you to my mum who is responsible for my self-esteem and resilience. She thinks her main contribution to this book was bringing me tea and coffee while I was writing, when actually it was her own youthful rule-breaking and ambition for me that made me capable of writing a book proposal in the first place.

And I would like to thank my dad who had a heart attack in the middle of my manuscript writing . . . which he hopefully does not attribute to proofreading his daughter's sex book. He proofread all my essays at university, continues to look over much of my reporting and can now also count editing my book as one of his achievements. Not bad for a troublemaker from the Debden council estate.